GLOBAL CYCLING NETWORK

This publication was made in collaboration with, and is published by, the Global Cycling Network ("GCN"). The GCN brand is owned by and associated logos are the registered trademarks of Play Sports Network Limited, a company registered in the United Kingdom at Chiswick Park Building 2, 566 Chiswick High Road, London W4 5YB, United Kingdom.

–

First published in Great Britain in 2022. All content correct at time of going to press.

–

Cycle racing and riders photography
© www.sprintcyclingagency.com, www.welloffside.com and www.swpix.com
Cover photography © www.sprintcyclingagency.com
Studio photography by www.jessewild.co.uk
Peter Stetina's Canyon Grizl image courtesy of Wil Matthews Photo

–

ISBN: 9781838235338

Printed and bound in Great Britain by Hampton Printing Ltd, Bristol

This book is printed on recyclable FSC (Forestry Stewardship Council) certified paper, which is sourced from sustainably managed forests, produced at a mill and printed by a printer that has been certified to the ISO 14001 environmental standard using vegetable oil based inks, and aqueous based coatings.

THE COMPLETE
FAN'S GUIDE
TO PRO CYCLING

EXPERT INSIGHTS ON THE RIDERS, THE RACES, THE TEAMS, THE TACTICS, THE LINGO & MORE!

PETER COSSINS AWARD-WINNING CYCLING AUTHOR

INSIDE THE WORLD'S TOUGHEST SPORT

Get a fuller understanding and greater enjoyment as we take you deeper inside road racing with *The Complete Fan's Guide to Pro Cycling*

Professional cycling is amazing and unique; a captivating spectacle quite unlike any other. It's often called 'the toughest sport', employing the latest technology and science, and demanding the highest levels of effort and commitment — yet exists in a culture steeped in history, romance and legend, with regulations, language and conventions that transcend time. That dichotomy can be as fascinating as the racing itself.

It's the only top-level sport where the world's biggest stars might come past your house, your workplace or your school. The incredible athletes of the men's and women's pelotons passing literally within touching distance as they bring their battle to us, on public roads.

The speed and sound, the blur of the brightly coloured jerseys and the sponsors' logos, the whirr of wheels and drivetrains, the support cars, the camera bikes, the commercial caravan. This cacophony surrounds the riders who generate incredible power, fight for victory on tiny margins and give everything in pursuit of their objectives... which may sometimes seem mystifying.

On the face of it, bike races are simple: all the riders set off together and the first across the finish line wins. But as soon as you scratch the surface, there are myriad stories, specialisms and sub-competitions to enrich our experience and — perhaps — confuse us. It's where riders hide their injuries or fatigue, sacrifice their own chances of success to support their team-mates, surprise their opponents with attacks, and give every last watt to close a gap... but then sometimes a leader may deliberately give up a jersey, or the peloton will allow a group to break away without trying to stop them. We'll explain why, and what to look out for.

In *The Complete Fan's Guide to Pro Cycling* we explain the different races, give insight into the many types of rider and reveal the tactics that go into making today's top level bike racing work — and who better to write this book for us than the award-winning author and journalist, Peter Cossins. He has an incredible ability to explain and illuminate the complexities of top level bike racing in an engaging but accessible way — and *The Complete Fan's Guide to Pro Cycling* will take you deeper than ever into our sport!

Dan Lloyd
GCN Director of Racing

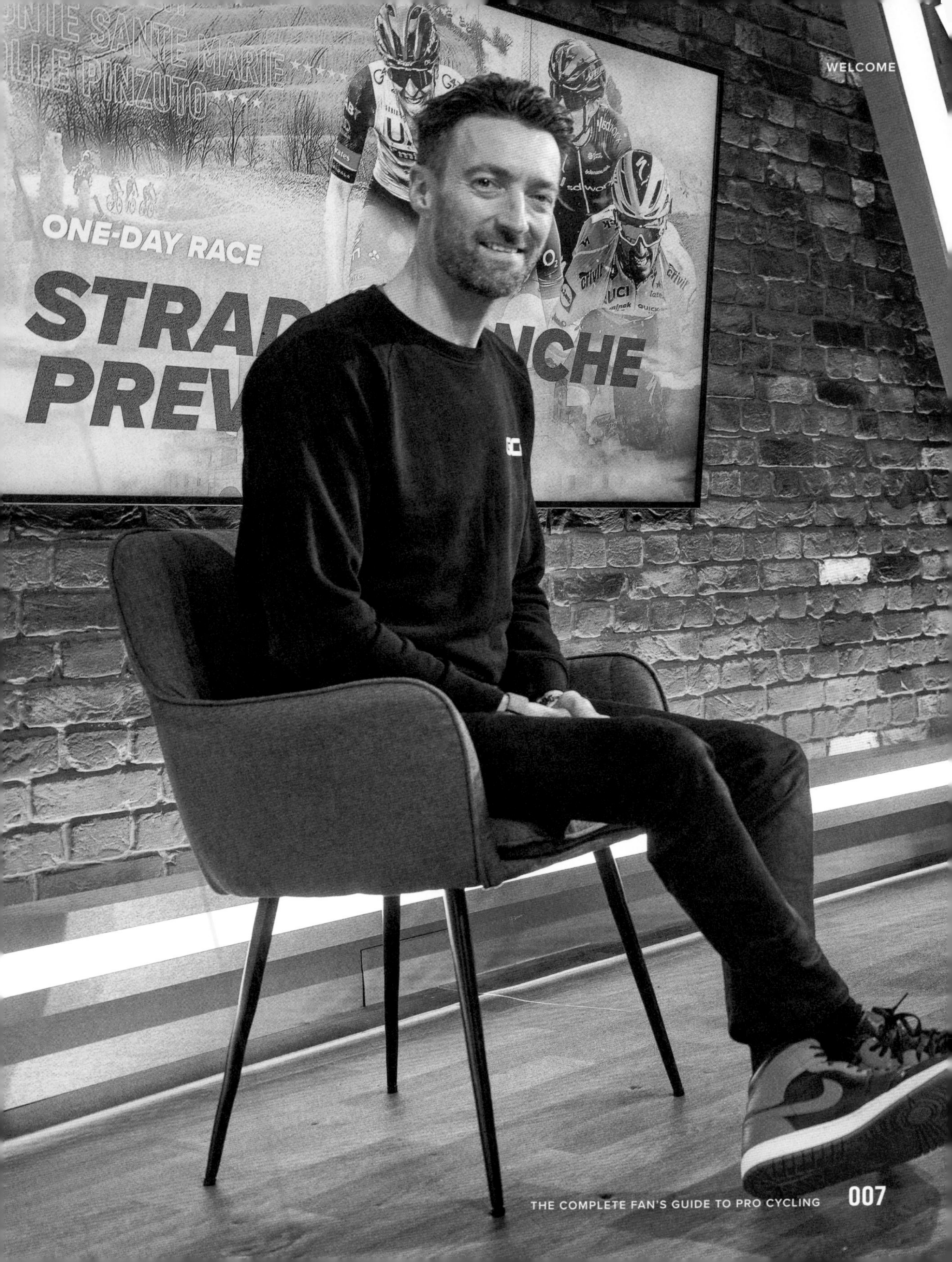
ONE-DAY RACE
STRAD
NCHE
PREV

ABOUT

WHAT IS GCN?

The world's largest community of road cyclists — with insight, expertise and entertainment from our ex-pro racer presenters

The Global Cycling Network (GCN) is the world's largest and fastest growing community of road cyclists, all bound together by daily entertaining, inspiring and informative videos, presented by ex-pro riders — from national champions in different disciplines to Grand Tour finishers — across YouTube, Facebook, Instagram and beyond.

Every day we create unique, informative and entertaining stories from all over the world of cycling to fuel your passion and knowledge for everything two-wheeled — all to help you become a better rider: from tech advice and know-how, riding skills, entertaining features, riding inspiration, racing, and more, you can find it and watch them all for free on GCN.

As well as our daily new video releases, we have thousands of videos already uploaded for you to discover, browse and watch whenever and however you want. GCN videos are as varied as how to fix your bike, what not to do on your first sportive or gravel race, epic adventures around the world, and what life's like as a pro racer — and much, much more. Our presenters offer a uniquely qualified look into the world of cycling, inspiring through their passion, humour and insight, and placing you at the heart of everything we do.

We also offer a premium service trhough our app, GCN+, where you can watch the best live racing all year round: live, and with expert analysis and highlights. The calendar is packed with hundreds of days of top-level men's and women's road, track and cyclo-cross racing, from Grand Tours to Classics and Monuments and much more besides. The races come with insightful commentary and exclusive analysis shows with former pro riders — from Adam Blythe to Sean Kelly to Pippa York, Bradley Wiggins, Dani Rowe, Robbie McEwan and other big names.

Alongside the racing you can watch the world's greatest collection of cycling films: original, exclusive, and all in one place. Find out more at **gcn.eu/discovergcnplus**

Did we mention that you can ride with GCN at our own events and festivals? That we have our own club delivering members exclusive sock designs every month? And did we mention that you can also find our content in Spanish, French, German, Italian and Japanese, as well as English?

If you like the sound of all that why not saddle up to discover more about us at **www.youtube.com/gcn**?

 /gcn   /globalcyclingnetwork   /globalcyclingnetwork   @gcntweet   gcnclub.com

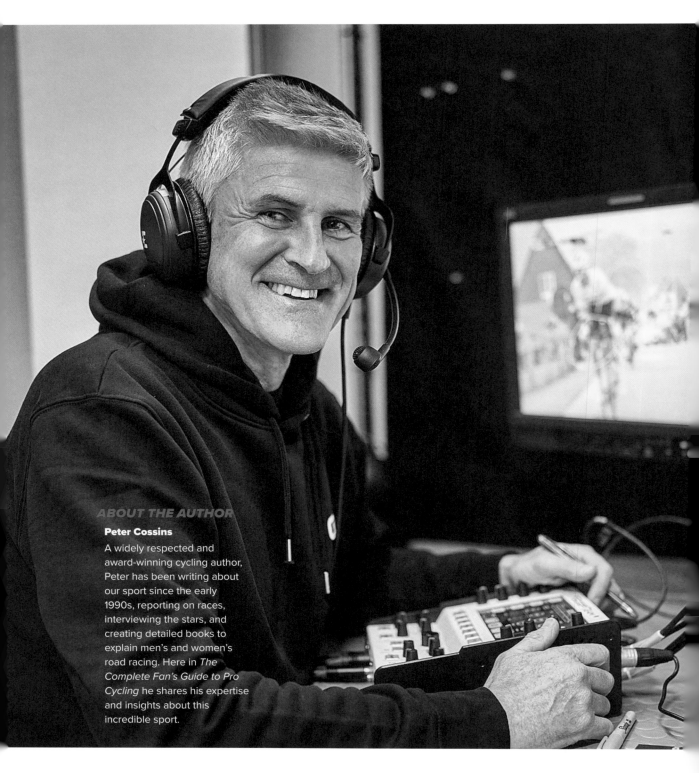

ABOUT THE AUTHOR

Peter Cossins

A widely respected and award-winning cycling author, Peter has been writing about our sport since the early 1990s, reporting on races, interviewing the stars, and creating detailed books to explain men's and women's road racing. Here in *The Complete Fan's Guide to Pro Cycling* he shares his expertise and insights about this incredible sport.

THE COMPLETE FAN'S GUIDE TO PRO CYCLING

CONTENTS

A multinational peloton passes under
Canadian and British flags flying over
Belgian cobbles on the Tour de France.
Confused? Don't be, come with us...

CHAPTER ONE

FUNDAMENTAL PRINCIPLES OF PRO CYCLING

As precision-plotted as chess, with as many bluffs as a game of poker, and as much adrenalin as you can handle, that's pro cycling

>> There are two fundamental truths about bike racing: firstly, as a sport, it's simple, yet complicated. The first rider across the line wins, but there are significant variables that can always impact that result — the type of race, the terrain, the weather conditions — as well as one elementary feature: that winner depends on the altruism of their teammates, who each play their own role in that victory, offering shelter from the wind, bringing food and water, enacting strategies, while at the same time thwarting the tactical schemes of rival riders and teams.

Secondly, freed from the confines of stadiums and arenas, it's spectacular. Races take place in every corner of the world, where astonishing scenery is not only the backdrop to the action, but frequently the setting for it.

"This book aims to lift the lid on this thrilling sport, helping to improve the viewing experience"

Added together, these two ingredients make bike racing one of the most exciting and dramatic of sports, capable of attracting as many as 2 million fans to the roadside on its biggest days. This book aims to lift the lid on this thrilling sport, highlighting race strategy (the macro take on racing) and tactics (the micro details that contribute to overall strategy), the races and their iconic locations, the bikes and kit, and the technology that's essential to success and that is, increasingly, helping to improve the viewing experience, too.

›

Drawing on the sport's illustrious history and interviews with contemporary racing stars – along with some of the management, racing tacticians and support staff who work with the riders – *The Complete Fan's Guide to Pro Cycling* aims to be the ultimate insider's guide to cycle sport, unpicking its hidden features, enabling you to understand what's happening in a race and what's likely to happen next, making bike racing even more compelling to watch. Ultimately, it'll reveal that there's always plenty going on in a bike race, even when it might appear that there's not.

HOW TO MAKE CYCLE SPORT HISTORY

Published in 1894, *La Tête et Les Jambes* – 'the head and the legs' – was cycling's first training manual. Written by journalist and future Tour de France founder Henri Desgrange, a rider of considerable repute who'd set the first officially recognised mark for the World Hour Record of 35.325 kilometres in May 1893, its title still encapsulates perfectly the qualities most necessary for any racer to succeed, even if its content has long since been superseded. Bike racing is as much about drawing on mental strength and nous, as it is taking advantage of physical prowess. To be successful, racers make the most of whatever physical resources they have when it's most important.

Or, as France's 1962 World Champion Jean Stablinski succinctly put it: "If you're strong, make everyone believe you're struggling. If you're struggling, make everyone believe you're strong."

Stablinski's quote underlines the significance and importance of the covert when racing, of riders keeping their cards close to their chest, bluffing their rivals, hoping to tempt them into making a rash move that might provide a winning opportunity. Bike racing is, essentially, poker on wheels.

The Frenchman personified these qualities. Although he rode for the most part of his career as a domestique (a rider who supports the leader – see more about this role in Chapter 4) committed to serving Jacques Anquetil, his illustrious team leader, 'Stab' was canny and capable enough to win his national title on four occasions, as well as the world crown.

More recently, Frenchman Thomas Voeckler was another rider who demonstrated how a quick tactical brain can compensate considerably ❯

WORLD HOUR RECORD

With a few format and regulation changes over the years – not least the UCI outlawing Chris Boardman's 'superman' position on a Lotus Type 110 – the kilometres ridden in one hour have stretched over the years.

MEN'S
2019
55.089
Victor **Campenaerts**

2000
49.441
Chris **Boardman**

1972
49.431
Eddy **Merckx**

1893
35.325
Henri **Desgrange**

WOMEN'S
2021
48.405
Joss **Lowden**

2000
45.094
Jeannie **Longo-Ciprelli**

1893
26.012
Mlle **de Saint-Saveur**

"Riders keep their cards close to their chest, bluffing their rivals... Bike racing is poker on wheels"

Victor Campenaerts set a new men's World Hour Record mark in 2019 in a Mexico velodrome

Before his five Tour de France victories, Jacques Anquetil broke Fausto Coppi's World Hour Record at the fourth attempt

French national champion and Grand Tour breakaway favourite Tommy Voeckler inspired fans in his homeland and way beyond

LEGENDS OF THE SPORT

JACQUES ANQUETIL

France's Jacques Anquetil was the first rider to win the Tour de France five times (1957, 1961-1964) and holds the record to this day alongside Eddy Merckx, Bernard Hinault and Miguel Indurain.

Anquetil was a powerful all-round cyclist but the basis for his stage-race victories was built on the time trial; in fact, so impressive was Anquetil against the clock that he earned the nickname 'Monsieur Chrono' (chrono meaning time trial).

for any slight deficit on the physiological side when he almost stole away with the 2011 Tour de France title by drawing on his racing nous and experience — he won stage 9 from a breakaway and held onto the leader's yellow jersey for 10 days. It's worth noting, too, that Voeckler's chance of victory evaporated when he became convinced he could win with his physical strength alone and threw away his tactical advantage. The head *and* the legs, Desgrange might well have reminded him.

STRATEGY IS EVERYTHING

These essential qualities are evident at every moment in every race. Take the breakaway group at the front, for instance. Some of the riders are likely to be almost fully committed, hoping that their collaboration will help their little gang stay clear of the big bunch behind. Others may be contributing a little, hedging their bets in case the break does get reeled in by the peloton, as is most often the case. There may even be riders who aren't contributing at all, either because they're following team orders or because they're hoping for a free ride.

Back in the peloton, meanwhile, the riders who are hoping to contend for victory will be sitting on the wheels of their teammates, staying out of the wind, and saving their energy. At the same time, those teammates will be focused on not only offering shelter but also maintaining a good position within the bunch; not too far up to be fully exposed to the wind, but not too far back in case there's an attack, a crash or, perhaps, a shift in the wind direction. The mental arithmetic is incessant, each rider calculating how to best save every possible watt of energy in order to preserve it for most effective use later.

> **"The riders who made the best use of their head and their legs will become evident"**

As the finish approaches, the results of those calculations become apparent. The riders who have made the best use of their head and their legs will become evident. This may happen some distance from the line, with one of the breakaway group dropping the other riders and soloing to victory. Or it might only become clear in the final few metres, as a sprinter who's been following the wheels almost to the last suddenly takes advantage of the watts they've saved by making an acceleration that's as well-timed as it is powerful — enough perhaps to push them over the finish line ahead of faster rivals who've slightly misjudged their effort and have revealed their hand too soon. ❯

WORLD CHAMPIONSHIPS AN ANNUAL HIGHLIGHT

The Worlds are a one-off, a race where head and legs matter, while birthplace matters even more. The best compete but it may not be the season's best who wins

In many sports, athletics and swimming among them, this is the blue riband event each season. Yet, while the world crown is highly prized in pro bike racing, largely thanks to the prestige that comes with wearing the champion's rainbow-striped jersey, it's rarely claimed by the season's best rider. This peculiarity stems from the unusual way in which the racing calendar was established and has evolved since early in the 20th century. At that point, racers seldom travelled abroad to compete. Just one event bucked that trend, Paris-Roubaix, the cobbled Classic race that was first run in 1896 and is still regarded by many racers and fans as the biggest one-day event of any season. Its inaugural edition was won by Germany's Josef Fischer and subsequent races featured significant numbers of Belgian riders.

CHARTING THE ROOTS OF CYCLE SPORT

With the establishment of the Tour de France in 1903, the calendar began to take shape. The first multi-day race held anywhere in the world, it was initially scheduled to run throughout June of that year. However, the prospect of being away from home for a month resulted in a sparse take-up by the leading racers of that era. Desgrange's decision both to postpone the event until that July and shorten it to 18 days – including two rest days in between each of the six stages – attracted 60 racers.

When it got under way, few rated its chances of success, even Desgrange himself. Yet, it quickly became a huge, popular sporting phenomenon, especially once it left Paris, drawing out thousands of fans, most of whom had never seen any kind of top-class sport before. The riders were acclaimed as heroes, and a boom in cycling participation and interest followed, encouraging Desgrange and other newspaper proprietors to set up other events. The Giro di Lombardia (Tour of Lombardy, now known as Il Lombardia) appeared in 1905, its sister one-day race Milano-Sanremo came two years later, followed in 1909 by the Giro d'Italia, Italy's national tour.

STAT ATTACK!
PARIS-ROUBAIX FINISHERS

The nationalities of riders who finished Paris-Roubaix reflect the globalisation of the sport over the last 100 years and more. It began as an almost exclusively local affair, now it's truly multinational.

■ French   ■ Belgian   ☐ Other

1896-1905

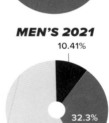

6.53%
17.84%
75.63%

MEN'S 2021

10.41%
32.3%
57.29%

WOMEN'S 2021

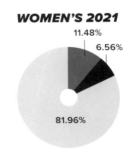

11.48%
6.56%
81.96%

The 1987 men's World Champion was the year's best rider: Ireland's Stephen Roche

INSTANT EXPERT

UNITED COLOURS

Five riders have won the Tour de France and the rainbow jersey in the same year:

Georges **Speicher** (1933)
Louison **Bobet** (1954)
Eddy **Merckx** (1971, 1974)
Stephen **Roche** (1987)
Greg **LeMond** (1989)

The other riders who have achieved this double over the course of their whole careers are: Antonin **Magne**, Ferdi **Kübler**, Fausto **Coppi**, Jan **Janssen**, Felice **Gimondi**, Bernard **Hinault**, Joop **Zoetemelk** and Cadel **Evans**.

THE SPRING CLASSICS LEAD INTO THE GIRO

By the outbreak of WW1, the racing season had developed a structure that's still familiar to fans in the modern era. One-day Classics such as Milano-Sanremo, Paris-Roubaix and, from 1913, the Ronde van Vlaanderen (Tour of Flanders) took place in the spring, followed by the Giro d'Italia (the Giro) in May and early June, the Tour de France (the Tour) in July, and then a further run of one-day races in the autumn, culminating in the Giro di Lombardia (Il Lombardia), the traditional season finale.

When the World Championships were first organised in 1927, they were slotted into a space on the calendar among what were by then well-established races. Rather than bringing the curtain down on the season as might be expected, they have almost always taken place in August or, more recently, September – albeit from 2023 the schedule moves back to August.

Although the world title quickly became a major target for the sport's best riders, winning the rainbow jersey has never gained anything like the same significance as taking the Tour's iconic yellow jersey, which has remained racing's greatest prize, largely because it's the one race of the year that brings in a huge non-cycling audience. Consequently, most of the sport's best riders, ❯

The last man to become road World Champion and later win the Tour de France has a one-day event – the Cadel Evans Great Ocean Road Race – named after him in his native Australia

especially its best stage-race exponents, tend to aim for a peak of form in July, hoping to put themselves and their sponsors in the sport's biggest shop window.

RACING FOR COUNTRY NOT TRADE TEAM

The 2021 World Championships road race in Leuven, Belgium, highlighted another issue that has meant the event's remained in the Tour's shadow. The men's race was won by Julian Alaphilippe, one of the pro peloton's star performers, in the blue, white and red colours of his native France. Organised by the UCI (Union Cycliste Internationale, cycling's international governing body), the Worlds have always been run under a national team format, with nations qualifying riders depending on results in other UCI-sanctioned races, such as the Tour, the Giro and the Classics. As a result, cycling's traditional powers, including France, Italy, Belgium, Spain and the Netherlands, usually field the maximum eight riders, while lesser cycling nations line up with half as many. The Worlds are a one-off, a race where head, legs and birthplace all matter. The length and difficulty of the race ensures that one of the best riders generally wins, but it's rarely the best rider of the season. That lack of predictably can add to greater excitement for fans, and for some interesting statistics to be thrown up over the years!

'OUTSIDER' WORLD CHAMPIONS

There are a number of riders who have won the World Championships road race but who were not really considered among the very best riders when they did – not least according to their UCI ranking: **Oscar Freire** was ranked 88th in 1999 when he took the rainbow bands, and in 2019 **Mads Pedersen** was 93rd. The phenomenon is shared by World Championships-winning women, but is not as pronounced. Among the lowest UCI ranked World Champion women are **Tatiana Guderzo**, 17th in 2009 and **Amalie Dideriksen**, 42nd in 2016.

In 2021 Elisa Balsamo became the first Italian women's road World Champion since the great Georgia Bronzini's back to back victories in 2010 and 2011

PETER COSSINS ON

THE IMPORTANCE OF THE WOMEN'S WORLDS

The World Championships Women's road race has a special status, having been running since 1958

On the women's side of the sport, the World Championships road race is one of the most established races on the calendar and is arguably the most prestigious. During the 2021 championships, Italy's Elisa Balsamo upset predictions of a fifth successive world title for the powerful Dutch team by outsprinting their leader, Marianne Vos, up the drag to the line in Leuven, Belgium. Despite the re-establishment of the Tour de France Femmes in 2022 and the first-ever running of Paris-Roubaix Femmes in the autumn of 2021, both events that are sure to boost the profile of women's racing, the Worlds should retain its pre-eminent position.

IT'S A TEAM SPORT

Riding as a team helps shelter leaders, climbers and sprinters so they conserve resources and are fully loaded to spring at the right moment

Cycling, it's often said, is a team sport where individuals triumph. There's perhaps no clearer evidence of this than the Tour de France winner offering the €500,000 prize to his teammates and his team's backroom staff to share between them in order to demonstrate his gratitude for their support over the previous three weeks. Although to put that apparently generous convention into context, it should be noted that the man who rides away with the yellow jersey will earn many multiples of this sum thanks to bonuses, endorsements and the inevitable rise in salary.

The dependency of one 'protected' rider on several others quickly became the norm during the sport's early years. This tactic was inherited from track racing, where it still features today in some events. On the road, the best riders would have a string of

STAT ATTACK!

TOUR DE FRANCE *Longest stages per decade*

DECADE	STAGE		DISTANCE
1900s	7	Marseille to Toulouse, 1906	480km
1910s	5	Les Sables-d'Olonne to Bayonne, 1919	482km
1920s	5	Les Sables-d'Olonne to Bayonne, 1924	482km
1930s	3	Nantes to Bordeaux, 1932	387km
1940s	21	Nancy to Paris, 1949	340km
1950s	21	Vichy to Paris, 1952	354km
1960s	21	Clermont-Ferrand to Fontainebleau, 1967	359km
1970s	9	Saarlouis to Mulhouse, 1970	269km
1980s	9	Nantes to Bordeaux, 1984	338km
1990s	5	Avranches to Rouen, 1990	301km
2000s	20	Belfort to Troyes, 2000	254.5km
2010s	15	Givors to Mont Ventoux, 2013	242.5km
2020s	7	Vierzon to Le Creusot, 2021	249km

INSTANT EXPERT
YOUNGEST TOUR WINNERS

At 19, **Henri Cornet** is the Tour de France's youngest winner, back in 1904.

In 2021, **Tadej Pogačar** became the youngest double winner, aged 22.

Above *Having dropped Alberto Contador and then bridged up to and dropped Nairo Quintana, Chris Froome heads for victory on Mont Ventoux in the 242.5km stage on the 2013 Tour de France*

"It's often said that cycling is a team sport where individuals triumph"

pacers at their disposal, usually seasoned racers happy to accept a guaranteed payday. They would wait at pre-arranged points on the route, where they would take on the pace-setting until the next rendezvous arrived. Inevitably, racing in this way skewed performance. The best-funded riders and teams had a significant advantage, especially when riders began to use two, three or even four pacers at a time. But it was a dangerous method, and became even more hazardous when riders began to use motorbikes and cars on unsurfaced roads that were either dry and very dusty or wet and glutinous. Accidents were frequent, fatalities not uncommon.

DISPENSING WITH THE PACERS

Once again, change came with the first Tour de France. Desgrange and his organising team opted to run the first five of the six stages without pacers — ultimately, they decided not to use them at all. While some manufacturers baulked at the initiative, most riders   ❯

Greg LeMond was as dominant in his USA colours, becoming 1989 World Champion, as he was in his La Vie Claire jersey winning the Tour de France

'The Professor' Laurent Fignon is almost as well known for his narrow loss to Greg LeMond in the 1989 Tour de France (8 seconds, the smallest ever General Classification margin) as he is for his two 'Grande Boucle' victories (1983, 1984)

A MAN FOR ALL SEASONS

If we're being generous and including criterium races, the record for the most months in which a rider won a race in a single calendar year was 11, achieved by GCN+ Commentator Robbie McEwen in 2002. The Australian sprinter only missed out on a win in the month of November!

hailed the levelling of the competitive playing field this provided. Even though there were no pacers to be seen when the Tour got under way on 1 July 1903 in the Paris suburb of Montgeron, the riders continued to race in the way they had become accustomed to, going off as quickly as they could from the start and gradually slowing, a process that would eventually leave those with most endurance at the front. Frenchman Maurice Garin proved the strongest of all, winning that first stage, which covered an enormous 467km to Lyon, and going on to win the title, partly thanks to the potency of his La Française team, whose riders filled the first five places in the final standings.

Gradually, the strategic approach to racing started to alter, and inevitably became more complex. Team managers and their leaders began to organise the roles of other team riders more rigorously, with the result that the peloton became a more cohesive unit, a place where the general classification (GC) leaders, climbers and sprinters could shelter and save resources until the moment when they judged it most effective to deploy them. This approach has evolved through the decades, but has essentially remained unchanged. Teams start each race or day of racing with a specific goal built around providing the best opportunity for success for the riders who are best equipped for the terrain and conditions that lie ahead.

"Team managers began to organise the roles of their riders more rigorously"

LEGENDS OF THE SPORT
EDDY MERCKX

Belgium's Eddy Merckx is widely regarded as the most successful cyclist of all time. Racing from the mid-60s to his retirement in 1978 he won the Tour de France and the Giro d'Italia five times each, the Vuelta a España four times, the World Championships three times, all five Monuments and many other Classics. His relentless style earned him the nickname 'The Cannibal'.

THE STRONGEST RIDER DOESN'T ALWAYS WIN

Having a physical edge on your rivals is always useful, but it does confer some responsibilities. Not only will you start as favourite and, therefore, right in the sights of every other team and rider, but it's likely that your team will have to take on responsibility for controlling the race, while the others sit in, watch and wait.

The Covid-affected 2020 season, when almost all of the major races were compressed into a thrilling three-and-a-half-month mash-up of Classics, Grand Tours and World Championships, provided extraordinary examples of how strength can enable a racer to prevail in spite of overwhelming odds and how it can become a burden that rivals exploit.

In the former category was Tadej Pogačar's Tour de France victory on his debut in the race. Although the young Slovenian began it tipped for a high finish, his UAE Emirates team looked, and ❯

consistently proved to be, under-powered in comparison to the Jumbo-Visma juggernaut supporting his compatriot and race favourite, Primož Roglič. Frequently isolated from his teammates on key climbs, Pogačar used Jumbo's strength to his advantage, effectively regarding them as his team and sitting in behind them for protection until the moments he needed to take on Roglič head to head. On the majority of these occasions, the Jumbo team leader came off best. However, when it mattered most, in the individual time trial on the penultimate day, Pogačar shocked many people – even himself – when he turned a one-minute deficit into a similar-sized lead. Just as Greg LeMond, leader of a very weak ADR team had done when he came through in the time trial at the very last to win the 1989 Tour, the young Slovenian racer had proved himself the strongest.

A month on from the end of the Tour, the finale of Belgian one-day Classic Gent-Wevelgem offered a perfect illustration of how being the strongest can sometimes prove counterproductive. Rivals Wout van Aert and Mathieu van der Poel were the favourites, but ended up neutralising each other. Sensing an opportunity, Mads Pedersen accelerated away from the small group containing this pair, bridged up to three riders just ahead and stormed past them in the sprint. "I tried to play it smarter than normal and it paid off," said Pedersen, while Van Aert and Van der Poel were both left complaining that the other had marked them out of it.

›

"Pogačar shocked even himself when he turned a one-minute deficit into a similar-sized lead"

LEGENDS OF THE SPORT

BERYL BURTON

Twice a World Champion on the road in the 1960s, Beryl Burton is amongst the most successful and inspirational female British cyclists. On the track she was World Champion for Individual Pursuit five times (12 times a medallist, a record that still stands). She was the first woman to break the hour barrier for the 25-mile time trial, and also went under 2hrs for 50 miles and under 4hrs for 100. Her 12-hour time trial record of 277.25 miles set in 1967 stood for 50 years.

STAT ATTACK!

POG VS ROG   *Time won and lost by Tadej Pogačar and Primož Roglič during the 2020 Tour de France*

STAGE	POG vs ROG	REASON	GC
4	Rog 0:04	Time bonus	Rog 0:04
7	Rog 1:21	Crosswinds	Rog 1:25
8	Pog 0:40	Pog attack	Rog 0:45
9	Pog 0:01	Time bonus	Rog 0:44
15	Pog 0:04	Time bonus	Rog 0:44
17	Rog 0:17	Pog dropped + Rog time bonus	Rog 0:57
20	Pog 1:56	Time trial	Pog 0:59

The rise of Slovenian cycling is personified by the thrilling battles between Tadej Pogačar and Primož Roglič

The pendulum of the 2020 Tour de France had seemed to swing Roglič's way until the very end. Fans got to watch every kilometre and every pedal turn of the drama as it unfolded

IT'S ALL ABOUT ENERGY CONSERVATION

Any relatively experienced cyclists will know the feeling of riding in a group and sitting behind another rider, 'soft-pedalling' for the most part. In that situation the biggest concern is not about getting left behind but, because maintaining forward momentum is so much easier, rather about the prospect of riding into someone's back wheel. As a consequence, when you move back to the front of the line, to set the pace for the rest of the group and, in turn, allow them to shelter from the wind, you've recuperated and as a result can push the pedals a little more firmly. Just like racers in the late 19th century, you've discovered the benefit and thrill of riding in a pace line, sharing the wind, the work and, crucially, the chance for recuperation.

"Group riding in a line, where you share the wind, the work and, crucially, the chance for recuperation"

For professional riders, that feeling of being hidden from the wind, of being able to spin the pedals rather than pound them, is fundamental to completing their competitive goals successfully and being able to comply with team orders. It is, essentially, their working environment. In a pro race, it's vital to save every fraction of energy, every watt, so that those resources can be employed in carrying out a specified role, in chasing down a break for your team leader, leading your sprinter out at the finish, or in making an attack when the time and the terrain suit you best.

BUT WHERE'S THE COMPETITIVE SPIRIT IN THAT?

As a cycling purist who wanted his races to pit rider and machine against rival rider and machine, Henri Desgrange didn't want to see racers drafting each other as he believed this distorted the value of the contest. As a consequence, he prohibited the riders who lined up in the inaugural Tour de France from pacing each other. However, as it was almost impossible to monitor what the Tour's participants were getting up to in between the control points dotted along the route of each stage, the riders opted for the path of least resistance, working with each other when they could and even providing shelter to team leaders.

In fact, even the reports in Desgrange's own newspaper, *L'Auto-Vélo*, made it clear that eventual winner of that first Tour de France, Maurice Garin, benefited in both of these ways.

›

A study in aerodynamic efficiency, QuickStep Floors won the Team Time Trial at the 2018 World Championships in Innsbruck

Domestique Dan, returning to his off-road roots – albeit not intentionally – at the 2011 Tour Of Qatar

Domestiques' duties are varied: Nic Dlamini rode the 2021 Tour de France in support of Fabio Aru, and here he's pushing the pace for Team Qhubeka at the 2021 Tour of Britain

THE SCIENCE OF SPEED

Gradually – and inevitably – acceptance of the peloton grew, even Desgrange recognising it was impossible to police infractions of any no-drafting rule. Although riding in a bunch can prove hazardous, its benefits more than make up for occasional perils, and recent research by Bert Blocken and his colleagues at the University of Eindhoven underlines how far these advantages extend.

Using quarter-scale models of riders placed in a peloton-like formation in a wind tunnel, Blocken's team calculated that every rider was saving energy to some extent, even the rider right at the front, who, unlike a solo rider, gains a little helpful assistance from the air being displaced forwards by the pack behind. Further back and into the heart of the peloton, the energy savings are far more significant, the research showing that riders in the middle of the group experience as little as five per cent of the drag of a solo rider. Even those riding on the front edges of the bunch experience between 60 and 67 per cent of the drag.

While the benefit of drafting is less pronounced in real life, where rider positions and the shape of the group are continually changing thanks partly to shifts in the wind and road direction, the reduction in the amount of drag remains substantial. Equally, this applies to smaller groups of riders, typically breakaways. The lead rider in a break will experience 98 per cent of the drag of a solo rider, gaining a slight 'push' from the riders behind, but the second rider experiences around 60 per cent of the drag, the third a little more than 50 per cent and the fourth a little less than 50 per cent.

> ## "The peloton is every rider's sanctuary, a place to hide until the right moment arrives"

Further research has shown that there's also substantial benefit from being in a pace-line on a climb, if the rider at the front is moving at a speed of at least 20km/h. This explains the well-established trend for the strongest teams to form 'trains' in the mountains, the front rider setting the pace until they're all but spent, a teammate taking over and the process continuing until, assuming they've judged their effort well, their leader can take up the running with a minimal number of rivals still on their wheel.

In short, the peloton is every rider's sanctuary, a haven from the harmful effect of wind resistance, a place to hide until the right moment arrives to put their nose in the wind.

›

MOST RIDERS WON'T WIN BUT HAVE A JOB TO DO

Pro cycling teams offer up a version of true team dedication, with some riders never personally experiencing a win but nevertheless being successful

Almost all racers enter the professional side of the sport with dreams of winning a Grand Tour title, a great one-day Classic or sprinting clear of a bunch with arms raised aloft, but less than half of elite male riders will have a win of any kind during the season (358 out of 802 in 2020 according to procyclingstats.com). What's more, some riders will go through a competitive career of maybe a dozen years or more and never once savour a personal triumph but will, nevertheless, look back and judge those years a success.

Going all the way back to 1903 Tour de France winner Maurice Garin and beyond, cycling's winners have always depended on fellow professionals putting them in the position to seize the sport's garlands. Prior to that first Tour, these racers would have earned their corn as *entraîneurs*, 'dragging' along those who had paid for their services – pace-makers in other words. As mentioned previously, Henri Desgrange did away with them when

JARGON BUSTER

DOMESTIQUE

From the French for 'servant', these riders look after their team leaders, sheltering them in the peloton, getting food, drink and clothing from the team car, even surrendering their own bike in the event of an irreparable mechanical fault.

Above A domestique is not just there to provide physical sustenance... Dani Martinez lifts Egan Bernal's spirits as he defends the lead of the Giro d'Italia

LEGENDS OF THE SPORT
JEANNIE LONGO

Five times road World Champion, and four times TT World Champion between 1985 and 2001, Jeannie Longo also claimed the Olympic road race gold medal in 1996 (and medalled in both 1992 and 2000). On the track the amazing Frenchwoman set the World Hour Record in 2000 after winning four World Championship golds in the 1980s across 3km pursuit and the Points race.

"Henri Desgrange maligned Brocco: 'He is unworthy. He is no more than a domestique'"

he launched the Tour and prohibited on-the-bike collaboration of any kind, but tacitly accepted it because it was almost impossible to police between check points.

SUPPORTING THE LEADER

During the 1911 Tour Desgrange took a stand against a rider he believed had made an arrangement with a rival. Frenchman Maurice Brocco was a decent professional who was backed by the Alcyon team that also featured 1909 Tour champion, François Faber. Having lost his own chances of victory in the Alps, Brocco, who had a reputation for such things, made a deal to help Faber on a subsequent stage. Desgrange got wind of the wheeze and disqualified Brocco, only for the rider to appeal the decision to the French federation, a move that enabled him to continue racing until his appeal was heard. Thwarted by this, Desgrange maligned Brocco in his newspaper *L'Auto Vélo*, declaring: "He is unworthy. He is no more than a domestique, or a 'servant'."

Brocco responded to the slur by winning the next stage through the Pyrenees, yelling barbs at Desgrange as he picked his way past riders to victory, only to see himself kicked off the race because this show of force supported the view that he had previously been working for Faber and not racing to his full potential. While Brocco had to leave the Tour and subsequently switched his focus to track, becoming one of the favourites of writer and track racing fan Ernest Hemingway, the term 'domestique' stuck. It became an integral part of cycling's lexicon, used increasingly not as an insult but to describe a rider who worked for a leader, sheltering them, finding food and water, and offering up their bike in the event of mechanical mishap.

SPECIFIC TYPES OF HELPER

In the modern era, there are several kinds of domestique, or *gregario* as they are known in Italy. They still protect their leaders from danger and keep them out of the wind, drop back to the team car to collect food or clothing, and pace them back to the peloton following a crash or mechanical incident. Strategically, though, they have much more specific roles, depending on their own qualities as a racer.

Some will focus on supporting their leaders during the initial hours of a race. Others are given the task of protecting their leaders ❯

"I was there!" Fans in replica kit and polka-dot T-shirts are within touching distance of their heroes making history

"The instant arrives that the whole team hopes will provide a pay-off for the legwork done earlier"

on the climbs, either by helping to set the pace on the front of the group or sheltering their leader within it. On days that are likely to end with a bunch gallop, some domestiques are designated to chase down the breakaway. On other days, they'll set up their sprinter for the finish, making sure their speedster is well positioned in the final kilometres, steadily ramping up the speed for them approaching the finish until, well inside the last kilometre, the final lead-out rider, known as the *poisson à pilote* or pilot fish, will lift the speed a little more. Here, the sprinter, like Mark Cavendish, will be tucked in on their wheel until the instant arrives when they launch an acceleration that the whole team hopes will provide a pay-off for the legwork done earlier.

In recent decades, the term 'super-domestique' has been applied to riders who have been or could be leaders but have, Brocco-like, decided to devote their considerable ability to a slightly more talented teammate, often in the mountains where   ❯

 **JARGON BUSTER**

COMMISSAIRE

A race referee who keeps riders and team staff on the straight and narrow, making sure they stick to the sport's rules and regulations, handing down fines and time penalties to rule breakers.

The first of Mark Cavendish's four stage wins at the 2021 Tour de France was the result of a Deceuninck-QuickStep team effort to chase down the lone breakaway rider, but the sprinter still had a lot of work to do

*As good as it gets! A French World
Champion, Julian Alaphilippe, winning
the first stage of the 2021 Tour de
France to claim the yellow jersey*

the biggest stage races are won and lost. Team Sky, now Team Ineos, have had a long string of these super-domestiques, Chris Froome starting out as one for Bradley Wiggins, while Richie Porte, Geraint Thomas and Michał Kwiatkowski fulfilled the same role for Froome. Jumbo-Visma then emerged with a cohort of their own, starring Wout van Aert, George Bennett and Sepp Kuss, rated by many as the best climber in the bunch but committed to setting the pace for Primož Roglič, Tom Dumoulin and Steven Kruiswijk.

For these super-domestiques, their finish is not at the line but at a pre-specified point on a climb where, after frantic pace-making, they will pull aside, coming to almost a complete stop having given just about every joule of energy they have. This skill is highly-prized, highly-rewarded and, unlike in Maurice Brocco's era, frequently received with extremely high praise.

A GAME BEING PLAYED

Prior to the start of any race or stage, the 20-odd teams taking part each have a briefing in their team bus, during which various members of staff will highlight critical points along the route, analyse how the weather conditions might affect the racing, outline possible tactics that will be employed by rival squads and, based on all this, lay out the overall strategy for the day. As the riders on all of those teams will have different strengths and the team directors will have an individual perspective on strategy, every team will start the race with a different plan of action. Seeing how those different plans unfold

> ## "Seeing how those different plans unfold and impact on each other is one of the beauties of bike racing"

and impact on each other is one of the beauties of bike racing. The sport is often described as being "like poker on two wheels", as each team attempts to decipher its rivals' moves while trying to conceal the cards that it's going to play at a certain point. Why is Team X riding near the front? Why is that guy from Team Y trying to get in the break? Should we tweak our tactics because Team Z has decided not to chase behind the bunch today?

Some team managers, though, believe the comparison with poker is not entirely fitting. "When you play poker, you can lose ❯

A former World Champion – as denoted by the small rainbow bands on the sleeves – Rui Costa performs road captain duties, discussing plans with his DS in the UAE Team Emirates support car

HISTORY IN THE MAKING

In 2022 Biniam Girmay became the first Eritraen to win a stage of the Giro d'Italia and the first black African rider to win a Grand Tour stage, reversing Mathieu van der Poel's stage 1 win on stage 10

everything on a single hunch," said Nicolas Portal, Team Sky's brilliant directeur sportif who oversaw nine Grand Tour victories before his tragic death, aged 40, in March 2020. He likened cycling instead to chess, explaining: "I prefer to play chess, so that when I get the riders to move and expend their energy, there is some thought behind that, a tactical plan. I don't want to play poker with them and risk the strategic plan for the whole team."

"When I get the riders to move, there is some thought behind that, a tactical plan"

A good example of this approach can be seen in the way that the team that is regarded as the prime favourite for victory, whether on the day or at the end of multiple days of competition, will often set the pace at the front of the peloton. Although this might sap the resources of some of their riders, it imposes control, allowing them to ride at the pace they choose, avoid the sometimes hazardous as well as mentally draining requirement to fight for position in the bunch and, most crucially, to be in the ideal position to react to any sudden changes in the racing situation.

A FUNDAMENTALLY NUANCED APPROACH

Within the peloton, each team will have a nominated road captain, almost always a highly experienced rider, who will make the calls on tactics, sometimes liaising via an earpiece with the head directeur sportif, travelling in the team cars behind the race, but often giving orders based on their racing knowledge. These instructions might be as simple as ordering a teammate to move further up the bunch because they're out of position or they could be a complete overhaul of strategy, perhaps due to the team leader being caught up in a crash or seeing an opportunity to take advantage of a rival team's leader suffering a 'jour sans' – a bad day.

Seeing and understanding these nuances in each team's tactical approach to the day's racing is fundamentally important. Those riders blessed with tactical nous will derive benefit from knowing when and where to best save energy, as well as when to attack or to chase down a break. Equally, spectators who become more aware of these tactical intricacies will not only savour the viewing experience much more, but will also, gradually, be able to predict what is likely to happen based on positioning and movement within the bunch and in breakaway groups. The fact that there's always a lot going on even when it might appear there's nothing going on will become increasingly apparent. ❯

JARGON BUSTER

DIRECTEUR SPORTIF

A directeur sportif (DS) is the man or woman charged with deciding a team's race tactics. Each team has several but the head has the final say.

THE RULES

Preventing cheating and accidents are the main drivers behind the remarkably few written rules professional cyclists have to abide by

In terms of what you can and can't do on the bike while racing, there aren't that many rules in pro cycle racing, in comparison with most other sports.

With regard to rider safety, the most fundamental rules require that riders hold their line when sprinting, that they compete on a bike that weighs at least as much as the UCI-regulated minimum of 6.8kg, that they wear a helmet, that hand slings between riders and pushing from team vehicles are prohibited. Also prohibited are riders receiving a push from a spectator, holding on to and drafting behind team vehicles, and any behaviour likely to bring the sport into disrepute such as throwing litter away outside designated collection areas or taking a natural break in front of fans at the roadside.

In reality, however, most of these rules have substantial grey areas, where rule infringements are either permitted or tacitly overlooked. Riders often drift to the left or right in sprints, but some leeway is usually allowed in interpretation of this rule as long as they are seen as not endangering the safety of others. Similarly, drafting behind team vehicles when they are in the race convoy directly behind the peloton is permitted, as is temporarily sheltering behind a team vehicle following a crash or a mechanical incident.

During the 2019 World Championships in Yorkshire, the UCI attempted to tighten up implementation of this restriction, which led to the controversial post-race disqualification of the winner of the under-23 men's world title, Dutchman Nils Eekhoff, after he was seen pacing behind a team car for a considerable period following an early race crash. Many riders condemned the decision, complaining that behaviour of this type was usually condoned. Although Eekhoff's disqualification wasn't overturned, the UCI's race officials, known as *commissaires*, have returned to a more laissez-faire response to this type of misdemeanour.   ❯

> **"In reality, however, most of these rules have substantial grey areas"**

💬 JARGON BUSTER

YELLOW JERSEY

The Tour de France's famous yellow jersey – the *maillot jaune* – is worn by the leader of the general classification. First awarded in the 1919 race, with the colour reflecting the pages of race sponsor's publication, *L'Auto*, it is the most coveted prize in cycle sport.

💬 JARGON BUSTER

STICKY BOTTLE

When a rider is handed a water bottle – or *bidon* – from inside a team car and the exchange takes several seconds, giving the rider a brief tow.

Collecting bidons from team cars is fine. Hanging on to them for too long isn't fine... but it is one of pro cycling's grey areas. Of course Canyon-SRAM's Tiffany Cromwell knows exactly what to do!

The peloton slows to pick up musettes at a feed zone in the 2019 Vuelta a España. This is not the place to launch an attack

At the 2017 Tour de France leader Chris Froome needed a bike change and Italian champion Fabio Aru attacked, before other riders advised him to – respectfully – back off

RESPECT THE RACE LEADERS

Mark Donovan

"I'd say 99% of the guys always stick to stuff like not attacking when the leader punctures or takes a natural break. The race leader always gets respect when they're moving around the bunch, as well. I'd also say that, 20 years ago, they'd have got even more but, nowadays, everyone's fighting for every position in every stage of a race. But an elevated level of protection is definitely still there."

JARGON BUSTER

FEED ZONE

Known as the *zone de ravitaillement* in French races, this is the area where soigneurs are permitted to hand up supplies in canvas bags known as musettes to their riders, who grab the straps as they ride by.

THE UNWRITTEN RULES

In terms of what you can and can't do on the bike while racing, as we saw previously, there aren't that many official rules in comparison with most other sports. However, while every sport has them, cycling has more *unwritten* rules than most others, that have evolved since the sport's inception, largely with the intention of encouraging an inbuilt attitude towards safety and, above all, a fair sporting contest.

» The sticky bottle: when riders drop back to the team car to pick up a water bottle, the unwritten rule allows them to hold on to the bottle for up to three or four seconds, the rider then pushing off from his team director's outstretched hand, taking the bottle as they do so. Linger any longer than this and the rider is in danger of being penalised for receiving a tow. The director will receive a sanction, too, for providing this illicit assistance.

» Don't attack when the race leader is having a 'natural break': this is a complete no-no, not only because the leader stopping indicates a temporary cessation of racing action, but also because many others in the peloton will see the leader stopping as their chance to do the same.

» Don't attack when the race leader has a mechanical issue: in a similar way to a football team playing on when a rival player is injured, this is seen as running counter to the spirit of the sport. Incidents of this type do happen, notably when Alberto Contador attacked race leader Andy Schleck after his chain came off during the 2010 Tour de France and, in the 2017 edition, when Fabio Aru attacked as yellow jersey Chris Froome was seeking mechanical assistance. In the first case, Contador got away with his brazen act, in the second Aru was chased down by other riders, who bluntly informed him he was out of order.

» Don't attack in the feed zone: these areas are regarded as a neutral zone, a short section of road, usually a kilometre or maybe two in length, where riders can pick up musettes – small canvas bags with long straps containing food and drink that are held out by team soigneurs. There are two reasons why: firstly, riders need sustenance; secondly, attacking in an area where team staff are doling out food-filled bags won't end well for someone.

» Pacing back in the convoy: as mentioned in the Rules section, this unwritten rule is actually the opposite of a written rule in the ›

UCI regulations. The unwritten rule allows pacing in the convoy, but at the discretion of the commissaire. "Simply because if you get a mechanical, it's not your fault," explains Team DSM's British rider Mark Donovan. "Often these things can be a bit of a lottery, when you get a puncture or something else breaks on your bike, and from our perspective we've put months and months of work into races and for something like that to ruin your racing would be unfair really. It's still hard to get back to the peloton... ok, it makes it slightly easier when you're in the cars, but you're still having a harder time than the guys who are in the bunch."

» Race neutralisation: this usually occurs if bad weather or a serious crash affects the race, or even a combination of the two, as was the case during the opening stage of the 2020 Tour, when sudden rain after a long, dry spell turned the roads around Nice into a skating rink. On these occasions, experienced pros (in 2020 Tony Martin was key) and the race leader signal a cessation of hostilities until conditions are seen as being safe for racing again.

» The race leader is allowed free movement throughout the peloton: their special jersey is a sign to the rest to allow them to pass unhindered, the peloton parting like the proverbial Red Sea.

» No attacking the race leader on the final stage of a Grand Tour: this is a peculiar one, not least because it's unclear why the rule developed, but it has become the norm in the modern era. Fans might expect it, especially when the time gaps at the top of the leaderboard are narrow, but the riders always call a truce, all but guaranteeing that the race ends with a bunch sprint.

CHAPTER 1 – FUNDAMENTAL PRINCIPLES OF PRO CYCLING
IN A NUTSHELL

As Tour de France founder Henri Desgrange highlighted in his training manual published in the 1890s, success depends on the head and the legs. While much has changed in the sport since then, that one essential truth remains paramount. The key to any victory is having the patience to play your cards at just the right time and then having the power to capitalise on your rivals reacting either too quickly or too late. It is a game of constant judgement and calculation, on the one hand trying to work out when and how other riders will attack, on the other bluffing in order to conceal your own intentions.

Riding down the cobbled Champs-Élysées in Paris: processional for the GC winner, and a prestigious, and often furious, competition for the remaining sprinters

The Netherlands' Ceylin del Carmen Alvarado can boast national, European and the 2020 CX World titles

CROSSOVER CYCLO-CROSS STARS

Riders who bring their skills and experience to bear in excelling in both road racing and cyclo-cross

WOMEN'S

Marianne Vos
Seven-time Cyclo-cross World Champion; 2012 Olympic road champion and three-time road World Champion

Pauline Ferrand-Prevot
2015 Cyclo-cross World Champion; 2014 road World Champion

Lucinda Brand
2021 Cyclo-cross World Champion; two-time national road champion

MEN'S

Wout van Aert
Three-time Cyclo-cross World Champion; six-time stage winner at the Tour de France

Mathieu van der Poel
Four-time Cyclo-cross World Champion; winner of 2020 and 2022 Ronde van Vlaanderen

Tom Pidcock
Cyclo-cross World Champion 2022; Brabantse Pijl winner, 2021

HEADING OFF ROAD

Cyclo-cross is enjoying a renaissance at all levels, nurturing some explosive talent that increasingly makes its way over into road racing

Also known as 'cross and CX, cyclo-cross sits in the gap between road and mountain bike racing. The bikes resemble road machines, but are set up with wider tyre clearances to prevent them becoming clogged with dirt. Heavier tread than road tyres provides greater grip and traction, and they feature lower gear ratios, too. As in mountain bike events, cyclo-cross riders essentially race as individuals on off-road courses.

Cyclo-cross does, though, differ from both of these disciplines in significant ways. It's a winter sport that takes place on courses that are usually less than 4km in length, and feature a variety of obstacles — steep banks and ramps, hurdles, off-camber technical sections, streams and ditches, sand and dunes, all of them designed to test their handling skills. Oh, and there's usually mud — sometimes an awful lot of it.

PERFECT WINTER SEASON EXCITEMENT

The elite cyclo-cross season, running from November to the end of January is focused on Belgium, where the sport is huge with three or four big events each week. Men's races last around an hour and are about 10-15 minutes shorter for women. Because cyclo-cross races are much shorter than road events, they demand far greater intensity, with participants racing at close to their limit throughout.

In recent seasons, it's been interesting to see how some of the top cyclo-cross riders have taken the road scene by storm, notably Wout van Aert and Mathieu van der Poel, both multiple winners of the world cyclo-cross title. The explosive power that's essential to off-road success transfers extremely well to certain kinds of road event, particularly those demanding a punchy, aggressive approach over a series of sharp climbs or brilliant handling on a tricky descent. Both of these riders are red hot in a sprint, too.

Cyclo-cross' popularity is surging, with races and participants appearing at all levels, and huge crowds flocking to the biggest events, creating a raucous atmosphere. As it's run on closed, off-road circuits, it provides not only great schooling for kids in every skill, but in a safe environment, too.

›

THE RISE OF GRAVEL

Gravel racing is growing at an astounding rate all over the world, merging attributes and skills from road, cyclo-cross and mountain biking

Gravel racing is a relatively new phenomenon, although it draws inspiration from the very early days of cycle sport when almost every road outside every town and city was unsurfaced. However, some races, including France's Tro Bro Léon, and sportives, notably Italy's Eroica, have long featured sections on gravel roads – itself a respectful nod to the roots of road racing. The latter triggered the establishment of the Strade Bianche race which is part of the WorldTour and Women's WorldTour calendars, and has quickly found a status with riders and fans alike, becoming an unofficial 'emerging classic'. But gravel racing first emerged as a discipline in its own right in the United States, where a quarter of the roads are unsealed.

As traffic levels increased, riders began to seek refuge on these dirt roads, venturing out with their cyclo-cross or mountain bikes. Their numbers grew and, inevitably, organised gravel races and rides soon followed. Among the first was the 340-mile Trans Iowa, established in 2004 by local cycling legend Guitar Ted. Two years later, a few dozen riders gathered in Emporia, Kansas, to ride through the Flint Hills. What's since become the Unbound 100 (see Chapter 3), formerly Dirty Kanza, now welcomes close to 3,000 riders.

"As the scene has flourished, pro racers and teams have been tempted in"

EMPHASISING PERSONAL CHALLENGE

The vibe at these races is laidback, with the emphasis on fun, adventure and personal challenge. The explosion in popularity of these events around the globe has been mirrored by the advent of the gravel bike, their drop handlebars and fat tyres revealing their origins in modifying and adapting road, cyclo-cross and mountain bikes, taking the most useful aspects of each of them – but also setting them apart as purposeful, pragmatic designs, which have become an important part of many bike brands' ranges. As the scene has flourished, pro racers and teams have been tempted in from road and off-road, and the UCI has launched a Gravel World Series featuring events worldwide.

INSTANT EXPERT

UCI GRAVEL WORLD SERIES

While there is some reluctance within an emerging scene that remains close to its grass roots, gravel racing is now formally recognised by the UCI. The Gravel World Series started in 2022, with events around the world – open to professional and amateur riders – with qualification to season-ending UCI World Championships races in the European autumn, where rainbow band jerseys are awarded in age groups.

Gravel racing has the biggest stature, and enjoys the biggest participations, in the USA

The general classification of the Tour de France is the biggest prize of the season – Tadej Pogačar won in 2020 and 2021 – but there are many other fine races to enjoy as well

CHAPTER TWO

THE RACING SEASON

You'll find exciting drop-bar action every week all through the year, but what's the season's structure, and when are the biggest races?

>> Up until the turn of this century, the road and cyclo-cross seasons dovetailed almost perfectly, the road campaign beginning when the cyclo-cross season ended in late January or early February and ending when off-road events were about to restart in mid to late October. Yet, since the UCI (Union Cycliste Internationale, the sport's international governing body) began to focus increasingly on the globalisation of cycle sport, the road calendar has stretched, with elite events scheduled across the first 10 months of the year, kicking off with the Tour Down Under and concluding with races in China and other points in the Far East.

This globalisation has been mirrored by regular overhauls and tinkering to the overall structure of the season. As the new millennium began, the UCI rankings were the only season-long measure of rider, team and national performance. At the same time, the leading one-day events were grouped into the World Cup series, which included the Monuments and other major Classics (which we'll explain in Chapter 3), as well as more occasional events such as the Leeds Classic in the UK and the Zurich Classic in Switzerland. Unlike the rankings, there was a jersey and financial prize on offer to the rider who finished atop the World Cup standings.

In 2005, this system was superseded by the establishment of the ProTour, which featured as many as 27 races, including all three Grand Tours and the other major stage races, the

INSTANT EXPERT

KEY RACES

The three Grand Tours, May's **Giro d'Italia**, July's **Tour de France** and August's **Vuelta a España**, dominate the northern hemisphere's summer. Also watch the Spring Classics and Monuments, Autumn Classics and the UCI Road World Championships in September just as cyclo-cross starts in the USA and runs through to the CX Worlds in January or February.

five Monuments and the other major Classics, plus a number of other races. Up to 20 teams were awarded licences to belong to the ProTour, which gave them automatic entry to all of these races. Event organisers were also granted a handful of wildcard spots that they could make available to other teams outside this elite. The ProTour system remained in place until the end of the 2010 season.

Subsequently, the ProTour and world rankings were merged and rebranded as the WorldTour, which comprised as many as 38 races, starting in Australia in January and often ending with a stage race in China. Like the World Cup, the leading rider in the series wore a distinctive jersey – or at least they did until 2018, when it was last awarded – and teams had to bid for and then hold licences in order to participate in WorldTour events, which still featured the season's major races. The teams at this highest level are now known as WorldTeams, while those in the level below them are ProTeams.

HUGELY PRESTIGIOUS, RANDOMLY PLACED EVENTS

Cycling's organisational structure has been complicated to follow. The one constant through all of this fettling of ranking systems is that the racing season's traditional narrative remains largely unchanged and, as a consequence, its fundamental and long-standing structural flaw is unaltered. Rather than building to a crescendo with its biggest event as the grandstanding finale, which is the case with most other competitive sports, pro cycling peaks in mid-season with the Tour de France, with lesser highs dotted throughout the year in the form of the Spring Classics, the Giro d'Italia, the Vuelta a España, the World Championships and the Autumn Classics. Thanks to this insistence on sticking with tradition, cycling resembles golf and tennis. They too have their long-standing, hugely prestigious, but quite randomly placed major events, the Majors and Grand Slams, respectively.

Remarkably, the season's structure does hang together, even though it might not seem coherent to new fans when they start

INSTANT EXPERT

WHAT'S A CLASSIC?

The Classics are cycling's biggest one-day races. Definitions of – and opinions on – exactly what makes a Classic vary, but being long established, long distance, hard and full of character are a good start. The majority are loaded to spring time, with another concentration in the autumn. Some are climbing-focussed, others are flat and favour sprinters. There are sub-groups within Classics, such as those based on location (Ardennes) or surface (cobbled). The most important ones are called Monuments.

Below *Lizzie Deignan's weighty cobble reward for soloing to victory on the 2021 Paris-Roubaix Femmes*

Whether a Grand Tour, a Classic or another type of race, they all have their own story for fans to savour throughout the season

"There is no single narrative to the season... no one rider can contend for all its major prizes"

INSTANT EXPERT
MOST WORLD CUP TITLES

Italy's Paolo Bettini won the most World Cup overall titles, with three consecutively, from 2002 to 2004, the final year of the competition. His feat included winning two Monuments: Milano-Sanremo and Liège-Bastogne-Liège, the latter also won by Sean Kelly, winner of the first World Series in 1989.

to savour the full richness of road racing beyond the Tour de France, its marquee event. Its quirks are accepted because, as fans quickly realise, there's usually a good reason for them. The Tour, for instance, sticks implacably to its July date because it coincides with the early weeks of the summer holidays in France. The Classics are the focus in the spring because tradition dictates, but also because due to being grouped close together they provide a story line of their own.

As this suggests, there is no single narrative to the racing season, but several, because no one rider can contend for all of its major prizes. Or at least that's not possible in the modern era when the science of training has raised the competitive level at every race between January and October. It's a smorgasbord of treats, each with a flavour that's a little different to the rest. It's complex, perhaps a little perplexing. Fundamentally, though, it works.

MAJOR MEN'S RACES

The road racing season stretches across nearly the whole year, with a winter off-season when cyclo-cross is the main competitive focus

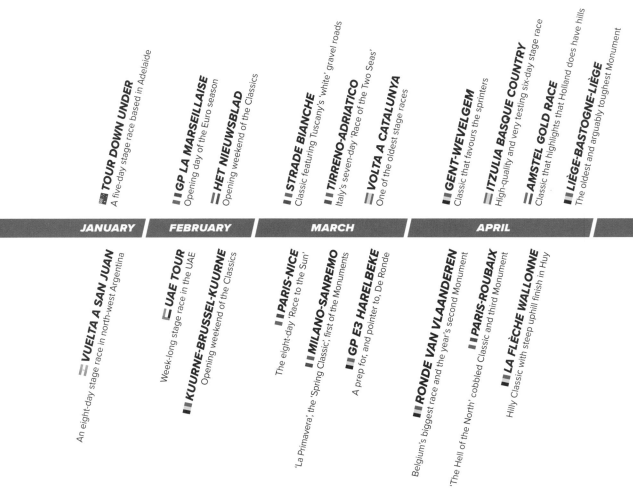

TOUR DOWN UNDER
A five-day stage race based in Adelaide

GP LA MARSEILLAISE
Opening day of the Euro season

HET NIEUWSBLAD
Opening weekend of the Classics

STRADE BIANCHE
Classic featuring Tuscany's 'white' gravel roads

TIRRENO-ADRIATICO
Italy's seven-day 'Race of the Two Seas'

VOLTA A CATALUNYA
One of the oldest stage races

GENT-WEVELGEM
Classic that favours the sprinters

ITZULIA BASQUE COUNTRY
High-quality and very testing six-day stage race

AMSTEL GOLD RACE
Classic that highlights that Holland does have hills

LIÈGE-BASTOGNE-LIÈGE
The oldest and arguably toughest Monument

JANUARY	FEBRUARY	MARCH	APRIL

VUELTA A SAN JUAN
An eight-day stage race in north-west Argentina

UAE TOUR
Week-long stage race in the UAE

KUURNE-BRUSSEL-KUURNE
Opening weekend of the Classics

PARIS-NICE
The eight-day 'Race to the Sun'

MILANO-SANREMO
'La Primavera', the 'Spring Classic', first of the Monuments

GP E3 HARELBEKE
A prep for, and pointer to, De Ronde

RONDE VAN VLAANDEREN
Belgium's biggest race and the year's second Monument

PARIS-ROUBAIX
'The Hell of the North' cobbled Classic and third Monument

LA FLÈCHE WALLONNE
Hilly Classic with steep uphill finish in Huy

GIRO D'ITALIA
The first Grand Tour of the season

CRITÉRIUM DU DAUPHINÉ
Week-long race in the French Alps

TOUR DE FRANCE
The second Grand Tour and biggest race of the season

CLASICA SAN SEBASTIAN
Basque Classic

GP QUÉBEC
Back-to-back Canadian Classics

TOUR OF BRITAIN
Week-long stage race

IL LOMBARDIA
'The Race of the Falling Leaves' and fifth Monument

| MAY | JUNE | JULY | AUGUST | SEPTEMBER | OCTOBER |

TOUR DE SUISSE
Eight-day race that's final prep for the Tour de France

VUELTA A ESPAÑA
The season's third and final Grand Tour

GP MONTRÉAL
Back-to-back Canadian Classics

WORLD CHAMPIONSHIPS
Staged over eight days in a different venue each year

TOUR OF GUANGXI
China's six-day race that brings the curtain down

MAJOR WOMEN'S RACES

*From 2022 the Women's WorldTour (WWT) has expanded out to include more races
than ever, as the women's sport moves towards parity with the men's*

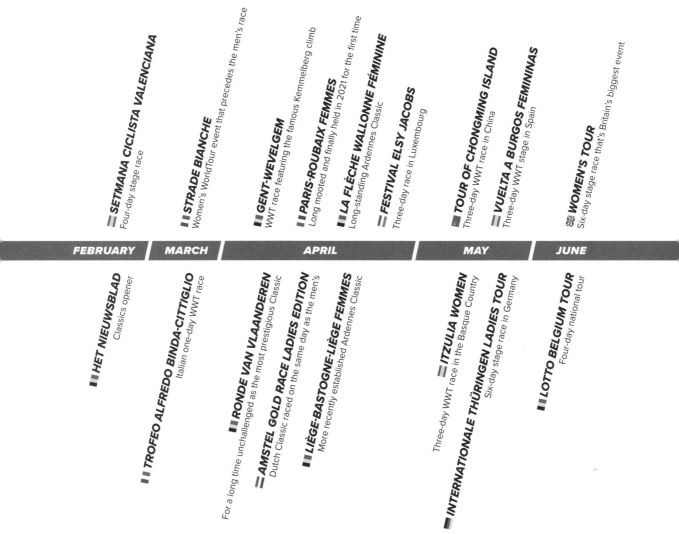

SETMANA CICLISTA VALENCIANA
Four-day stage race

STRADE BIANCHE
Women's WorldTour event that precedes the men's race

GENT-WEVELGEM
WWT race featuring the famous Kemmelberg climb

PARIS-ROUBAIX FEMMES
Long mooted and finally held in 2021 for the first time

LA FLÈCHE WALLONNE FÉMININE
Long-standing Ardennes Classic

FESTIVAL ELSY JACOBS
Three-day race in Luxembourg

TOUR OF CHONGMING ISLAND
Three-day WWT race in China

VUELTA A BURGOS FEMENINAS
Three-day WWT stage in Spain

WOMEN'S TOUR
Six-day stage race that's Britain's biggest event

FEBRUARY	MARCH	APRIL	MAY	JUNE

HET NIEUWSBLAD
Classics opener

TROFEO ALFREDO BINDA-CITTIGLIO
Italian one-day WWT race

RONDE VAN VLAANDEREN
For a long time unchallenged as the most prestigious Classic

AMSTEL GOLD RACE LADIES EDITION
Dutch Classic raced on the same day as the men's

LIÈGE-BASTOGNE-LIÈGE FEMMES
More recently established Ardennes Classic

ITZULIA WOMEN
Three-day WWT race in the Basque Country

INTERNATIONALE THÜRINGEN LADIES TOUR
Six-day stage race in Germany

LOTTO BELGIUM TOUR
Four-day national tour

WOMEN'S TOURS

The women's season differs significantly to the men's when it comes to stage races

There used to be a Tour de France Féminin, but that gradually faded from view, and Tour de France organisers relaunched the event in 2022. Italy has long had a Grand Tour, the Giro Rosa, which currently runs across 10 days. Although it's regarded as the biggest stage race of the season, it's been beset by financial and organisational issues and was dropped from the Women's WorldTour calendar in 2021. The Vuelta organisers have established a women's race, extending it to five days in 2022.

Races that could develop to become Grand Tours have emerged outside the traditional nations. Britain has the Women's Tour, Norway its Ladies Tour and the Netherlands the Boels Tour.

TOUR DE FRANCE FÉMININ AVEC ZWIFT
Eight-day stage race established in 2022

POSTNORD VARGARDA WEST SWEDEN
WWT team time trial and road race on consecutive days

BOELS LADIES TOUR
Six-day stage race

CERATIZIT CHALLENGE BY LA VUELTA
Five-stage national tour

WORLD CHAMPIONSHIPS
The biggest races of the season staged over eight days

GP BEGHELLI
Italian one-day race

JULY	AUGUST	SEPTEMBER	OCTOBER

GIRO ROSA
Italy's 10-day stage race – the toughest of the season

LADIES TOUR OF NORWAY
Four-day stage race

GP DE PLOUAY
One-day WWT event on rolling terrain in western France

TOUR CYCLISTE DE L'ARDÈCHE
Week-long stage race in southern France

TOUR OF GUANGXI
Chinese one-day race that concludes the WWT

In Richmond, Virginia, in 2015, Slovakia's Peter Sagan won the first of three successive World Championship titles, catapulting him to superstardom

2021 World Champion Elisa Balsamo celebrates with Italian team-mates after beating Marianne Vos in a sprint

WHAT ARE THE WORLD CHAMPIONSHIPS?

One-day races for the year's title and earning the right to wear the prestigious rainbow bands

Held in early autumn, the World Championships take place across eight days, encompassing time trial (TT) and road races for elite, under-23 and junior men and elite and junior women. Organised by the UCI, the events are run along national rather than trade team lines, countries qualifying riders depending on the results and ranking points earned during the previous season.

Until 1995, the championships were split between professional and amateur categories, but since then they have featured solely elite-level races for men and women, as well as the under-23 and junior events. Jerseys bearing the rainbow bands are awarded to the world champions in each race. Those riders are then permitted to wear their rainbow jersey for the following year when racing in the category and discipline in which they took the title. So, the elite road champions can wear their colours in road events, the time-trial winners in TTs.

"I absolutely love wearing this jersey... I really want to enjoy it, to make the most of it from the first day to the last"

Elisa Balsamo, UCI Elite Women Road World Champion, 2021

The other primary difference between the Worlds and most other races is that the events generally take place on a closed circuit, the racers lapping it several times. Some recent hosts (Innsbruck 2018, Yorkshire 2019, Flanders 2021) have slightly adapted this by arriving at the closed circuit from a different start point for each race, effectively spreading the World Championship love a little further around the region hosting the event.

For the riders, the Worlds and the rainbow jersey matter because they get to race in it for a whole season. "It's the most beautiful of jerseys," said 2020 and 2021 world road-race champion, Julian Alaphilippe. "It's a privilege to wear the world champion's jersey in the world's most prestigious races."

"It's a privilege to wear the world champion's jersey in the world's most prestigious races"

Julian Alaphilippe, UCI Elite Men Road World Champion, 2021

Even when the jersey passes to another rider, the bands stay with the former champions, who have the right to wear them on the sleeves of their jersey. ❯

THE OLYMPIC TITLES

One-day race every four years where cycling's elite from many nations rub shoulders with stars from other sports

Although there has been a men's road race on the Olympic programme since the inaugural Athens Games of 1896, the event has only been open to professionals since 1996, when Switzerland's Pascal Richard won the gold medal ahead of Denmark's Rølf Sørensen and Britain's Max Sciandri. The road time-trial event was reintroduced that year, Miguel Indurain winning the title ahead of his Spanish compatriot Abraham Olano, while Chris Boardman took bronze for Britain.

Since then, cachet associated with the Olympic title has grown immensely. Following his road-race win in Rio de Janeiro in 2016, Belgium's Greg Van Avermaet rode on a gold-painted bike, with a golden helmet and, of course, with the Olympic rings on the ends of his sleeves! Its importance can be gauged still further by the fact that the Olympics is, along with football's World Cup, the only other sporting event that carries enough weight to force the Tour de France out of its traditional July slot.

DRAMATIC RACING

Delayed by a year because of the Covid pandemic, the road-race events at the 2020 Tokyo Olympic Games produced two surprise winners in Ecuador's Richard Carapaz and Austria's Anna Kiesenhofer. Carapaz's coup gave his country what was only its second gold medal in Olympic history, while Kiesenhofer's success was even more of a shock because the Austrian was in the early break and managed stay clear despite a frantic – too late – chase by the title favourites.

Olympic success is, arguably, more significant for the leading women racers because, in the absence of a race that draws an audience beyond committed bike fans in the way the Tour de France does, it's the only opportunity they have to take centre stage in world sport.

"Back in my country they'll be going crazy because this is just the second gold in our history. It's special because it's the first in this sport and I think cycling's the sport that most people follow in my country"

Richard Carapaz, Olympic Road Champion, Tokyo 2020

Ineos Grenadiers' Richard Carapaz rides a gold bike with a gold helmet to celebrate his Olympic success

PRO'S PERSPECTIVE

WINNING AN OLYMPIC TITLE IN RIO!

Anna van der Breggen has won almost everything in cycling – and the 2016 Olympics remains a highlight

>> "It was the hardest parcours that we'd ever had for a one-day race. It had everything. Coastline, wind, pretty bad cobblestones, especially at the beginning; small climbs that were hard and steep, downhills, and it was almost 140km long. So it was a long, tough race, but I knew it was an opportunity I may never have again...

"Everyone knew that the last climb was the hardest, so I thought that to have a chance I should go before. It was a nice but painful climb, and the downhill pretty technical.

"After a race that hard you can't sprint any more, especially after the chase we did to bring back Mara Abbott. In the moment, you realise you've won the Olympics, but that didn't really matter if Annemiek wasn't alright [Annemiek van Vleuten crashed into concrete banking 10km from the finish]. When I heard that, actually, she was OK... that was the moment I realised it wasn't just the four of us who had raced to the finish line, it wasn't just the Dutch team, it was all the people in Holland who were watching. That feeling was really special."

THE TRIPLE CROWN AND OTHER ACCOLADES

The greatest riders combine major race wins to create historic palmarès... but what do they mean?

Cycling's Triple Crown describes Irishman Stephen Roche's victories in the Giro d'Italia, Tour de France and World Championship in 1987. This hugely impressive achievement was only previously matched by Eddy Merckx and, subsequently, by no one else at all. A case is made for including wins in the Tour, the Vuelta a España and the Worlds, as the Spanish Grand Tour has increased in stature over recent decades.

A similar term is used to describe victory in each of the three Grand Tours, which features a larger but still very select group comprising Jacques Anquetil, Felice Gimondi, Merckx again, Bernard Hinault, Alberto Contador, Vincenzo Nibali and Chris Froome – Hinault and Contador get particular kudos for winning each of the Grand Tours at least twice.

The distinction could equally be applied to those riders who have held all three Grand Tour titles at the same time. Eddy Merckx achieved this outstanding feat by winning the Giro and Tour in 1972 and the Vuelta in 1973, the latter then taking place in an April/May date rather than its current September slot. 'The Cannibal' even managed to extend this run by successfully defending his Giro crown in 1973. The only other riders to emulate the great Belgian are Frenchman Hinault, who claimed the 1982 Giro and Tour followed by the 1983 Vuelta, and Britain's Froome, who won the Tour and Vuelta in 2017 followed by the 2018 Giro.

WINNING ALL FIVE MONUMENTS?

The Monuments are the five most prestigious one-day Classics, the term originating during the UCI's reorganisation of the allocation of ranking points and used to set them above the other one-day Classics in the hierarchy. Just three riders have won all five: Merckx, Rik Van Looy and Roger De Vlaeminck. Merckx is in a class of his own, winning all five at least twice. All three are Belgian, underlining the country's special affinity with the Classics.

Three riders have come close to joining this illustrious trio. Sean Kelly won four and was runner-up in the Ronde van Vlaanderen

STAT ATTACK!

TRIPLE CROWN WINNERS... & NEARLY MEN

There are only two true Triple Crown winners in cycling history: Eddy Merckx in 1974 and Stephen Roche in 1987. But other great riders have come close, not least Miguel Indurain in 1993 when he did the Giro d'Italia/Tour de France double and finished second behind Lance Armstrong at the World Championships in Oslo. Greg LeMond finished third in the Giro and second in both the Tour and the Worlds in 1985. And in 1949, Fausto Coppi did the Giro/Tour double and finished third at the World Championships.

In recent years, Tom Dumoulin wasn't far off in 2018, although he didn't win any of them. He finished second in both the Giro and the Tour (only the third rider in history to do that after Gino Bartali in 1949 and Claudio Chiappucci in 1992) and then managed a fourth place at the Worlds.

Roger De Vlaeminck is one of just three riders – all Belgian – to have won all five Monuments

LEGENDS OF THE SPORT
ALBERTO CONTADOR

Along with Eddy Merckx, Contador is the only rider to win all three Grand Tours more than once: two Tours, two Giros, and three of his home tour, the Vuelta a España. It would have been three of each if it wasn't for being stripped of titles after testing positive for clenbuterol. 'El Pistolero' (named for his quickfire, attacking style) was a superb climber, winning the final mountain stage atop the iconic Angrilu on his final Vuelta campaign in 2017.

on three occasions. Dutchman Hennie Kuiper missed out on Liège, finishing second there in 1980, while Fred De Bruyne's second place at Il Lombardia in 1955 left him so close to joining his Belgian compatriots at the top table. Note that it's only been possible for women racers to win a maximum of two Monuments. Milano-Sanremo was the first to establish a women's race in 1999, with De Ronde in 2004. The Italian race was abandoned after 2005, Liège eventually filling that void in 2017. The inaugural Paris-Roubaix Femmes took place during the spring of 2021.

CHAPTER 2 – THE RACING SEASON
IN A NUTSHELL

Freeform in its formation, the road-racing calendar has defied almost every attempt to establish an instantly understandable narrative. Essentially, the Tour de France took a central position in the calendar and every race that has appeared since has had to work around this unmovable behemoth that draws in the best riders, the most fans and the highest viewing figures. Nevertheless, the calendar does hang together well, with a Monument towards the start and finish, the World Championships towards the end, and plenty of quality road racing throughout the 10-month season.

The CX World Championships comes at the end of the intense cyclo-cross season, just as many riders – such as 2022 winner Tom Pidcock – are preparing for their road season

THE CYCLO-CROSS SEASON

As autumn approaches the dirty side of drop-bar racing comes to the fore, with top-level 'cross competition

Although there are races as early as September, bike racing's winter discipline gets fully into gear from mid-October, just as the road season is winding down. There are three principal international competitions: the UCI-organised World Cup, the long-standing and prestigious SuperPrestige series, and the X2O Badkamers Trofee that was established by and known for many years as the Gazet Van Antwerpen Trofee.

The CX scene is heavily focused on Belgium, where the sport has a large and enthusiastic fan base. The majority of the World Cup and SuperPrestige events take place here, as do all of the races that comprise the X2O Badkamers Trofee. The season culminates with the World Championships in late January or early February, which have a much broader scope. Although the 2021 championships took place at Ostend in Belgium, the 2022 championships were held at Fayetteville in the USA, while the 2023 championships will take place at Hoogerheide in the Netherlands, followed by Tábor in the Czech Republic in 2024 and Liévin in France in 2025.

INSTANT EXPERT

ORIGINS OF CYCLO-CROSS

Cyclo-cross has its roots at the start of the 20th century, emerging in France in local competitions where riders would compete to reach local landmarks (known as 'steeple chasing'), with their bikes by any reasonable means!

The first French National Cyclo-cross Championships took place in 1902, with the sport spreading to its heartland of Belgium, and other neighbouring European countries. The first Cyclo-cross World Championships was in 1950 with the first USA Cyclo-cross National Championships in 1964.

The gravel racing calendar, growing internationally, retains a more fluid structure, reflecting the sport's underlying characteristic

THE GRAVEL SEASON

Gravel racing is growing quickly and some of the existing events are becoming UCI-sanctioned

The gravel calendar has evolved organically, away from any consolidating structure, which is entirely in keeping with the kitchen-table organisation of these events, where the focus has been on racers going back to the sport's free-roaming roots, the emphasis firmly on challenge and fun. The scene has largely developed in the US, where there are gravel events pretty much every weekend all year. At the biggest, including Unbound Gravel, SBT GRVL, the Belgian Waffle Ride, the Mid South and Rebecca's Private Idaho, 'the Monuments of Gravel' as dubbed by US magazine *Velonews*, thousands of places can sell out in minutes (see page 115).

"At the 'Monuments of Gravel', thousands of places can sell out in minutes"

While the UCI has announced its intention to introduce a World Gravel Championship, and has unveiled a Gravel World Series aimed at including both professionals and age-group enthusiasts, there is a strong feeling in many amongst the gravel community that they don't need to be sanctioned by the ruling body.

CHAPTER THREE

THE RACES

Why are the Grand Tours so grand? What's a Classic and what's a Monument? How do the men's and women's racing calendars compare?

>> With cyclo-cross season being the drop-bar racing highlight of the northern hemisphere winter, road racing season has extended out from its traditional schedule in Europe's milder seasons as it has developed an increasingly global presence. Fans can now enjoy WorldTour season openers in the Australian summer followed by races with growing stature in the Middle East, as the calendar offers us a seemingly non-stop series of entertainment. But which are the best races, the biggest, the most important and the most entertaining?

STAGE RACES EXPLAINED
Before looking at specific stage races, let's start with an explanation of how they work

Stage races are multi-day events that last anything from two to 24 days, with most falling into the bottom end of that range. As many as two dozen teams comprising between five and eight riders, depending on the length and status of the event, compete over a series of stages — a minimum of three (races can have two stages on one day, although this is now rare) and a maximum of 21, plus a prologue time trial in the case of the three-week Grand Tours, which also have rest days built into their schedule.

Essentially, there are two races going on within the one event: the contest for the stage win and the longer battle to be the overall winner of the race. The former is easy to grasp; the first rider across the line is the winner. Each rider will be given a finishing time. For those who are in the same group or peloton as the victor — assuming there are no significant splits — it will be the same time as the first rider.

>

INSTANT EXPERT
WHAT'S A GRAND TOUR?

Three-week races that encompass all the glory and the pain of European geography, the three Grand Tours are the **Tour de France**, the **Giro d'Italia** and the **Vuelta a España**. The Tour de France is, without doubt, one of the largest and most fervently supported spectator sports in the world.

Approaching the summit of the iconic climb, Col du Tourmalet, FDJ's Thibaut Pinot checks back on the yellow jersey, Julian Alaphilippe

As races progress, each rider builds up a cumulative finishing time, with the race leader's jersey (with a distinctive bright colour), awarded to the rider with the lowest overall time. This leads to the counterintuitive eventuality of riders who often appear to be dominating a race by winning several stages (bunch sprinters such as Mark Cavendish, for example), being well out of contention for the leader's jersey and overall victory. They're good on certain days, but either don't have the consistency or the all-round ability to be in contention on almost every day.

STAGES THAT SUIT DIFFERENT RIDERS' STRENGTHS

Stage race specialists, or general classification (GC) riders as they're also known, need to be strong on the flat, in the hills and in time trials. They're usually blessed with plenty of tactical know-how, too. Any rider who's deficient in one of those areas will struggle to contend for the overall victory. As a consequence, they're likely to focus on the specific stages that suit their strengths – bunch sprints for Cavendish and his fast-finishing rivals, time trials for specialists such as Filippo Ganna, and mountain stages for the pure climbers.

> ## "Bunch sprints for Cavendish and Co, time trials for specialists such as Filippo Ganna, and mountain stages for the pure climbers"

The terrain, weather, distance, format and strength of the field are guarantees that every stage race will be different. Sometimes those differences will be only slight, but occasionally others are significant and then the racing will be different, too. To offer an example, a three-week Grand Tour such as the Tour de France features all of the WorldTeams that are at the top level of the sport's hierarchy, plus a few 'wildcard' picks from the next level down. Because of the prestige of the event, each of these teams will select its best riders, ideally those who are reaching the peak of their form, with the result that the overall level will be at its highest point all year.

However, a couple of rungs down the organisational ladder at a 2.1-categorised race such as France's Route d'Occitanie, the number of days of racing and the quality of the teams and riders will provide a different kind of test and spectacle, frequently with racing that can be more unrestrained and exciting. ❯

CONOR'S FAVOURITE RACES

"My favourite one-day race as a pro – that's Milano-Sanremo... the history, the journey and the sheer 'epicness'. You feel like you've covered a country in a day. And then there's the beautiful postcard finish in Sanremo itself.

"My favourite stage race is probably the Giro d'Italia for the passion of the crowds and the food along the way.

"I also loved any race in Australia for the cafe stops pre-race and racing in Asia for the beauty, and sense of being in a totally different place that I admit I probably wouldn't get to see if it wasn't for the bike race."

💬 JARGON BUSTER
PELOTON

The French word for 'bunch' (amongst other things) that's now commonly used by fans and commentators across the world.

COMPETITIONS WITHIN COMPETITIONS

In stage races, besides the General Classification, there are multiple smaller competitions also going on. They vary from race to race, can also change over time, and the leaders and final winners are usually denoted by being awarded a specific jersey.

GENERAL CLASSIFICATION

At the end of each day the jersey is awarded to the rider with the lowest cumulative time. The rider at the end of the final stage in the lowest overall time is the GC winner.

POINTS CLASSIFICATION

Points for are awarded for the highest placed finishers on each stage, regardless of time gaps. There are more points on flat stages, and so they're often contested by sprinters.

MOUNTAINS

Points are awarded as riders summit certain climbs, which are categorised 4, 3, 2, 1 and, in the Tour de France and Vuelta a España, *hors catégorie*, for the most difficult.

YOUNG RIDER

Works in the same way as the General Classification, but it is only open to riders aged 25 or under. A recent phenomenon is more younger GC riders winning both.

TEAM CLASSIFICATION

Calculated by adding together the times of a number of riders on each team on each stage (usually the first three); the leading team is the one with the lowest cumulative time.

COMBATIVITY AWARD

After each stage a jury decides who to reward as the most aggressive rider – often those in breakaways. A 'super-combativity award' is given at the end of the race.

| GIRO D'ITALIA | TOUR DE FRANCE | VUELTA A ESPAÑA |

With an adrenalin spike thanks to the noisy fans, Team DSM's Romain Bardet climbs to stage victory in the Vuelta a España

MAY	JULY	AUGUST

GRAND TOUR CALENDAR

The three big-hitters of the men's road racing calendar each dominate a month of the cycling summer

GIRO D'ITALIA
The first Grand Tour of the season, raced since 1909

TOUR DE FRANCE
The second Grand Tour and biggest race of the season

VUELTA A ESPAÑA
The season's third Grand Tour, and often the hottest and most mountainous

COMBINED CLASSIFICATION

Historically, the Grand Tours have run a Combined Classification, by tallying up the riders' positions in the GC, points, and mountains. The Tour de France ran its competition between 1968 and 1989 (Eddy Merckx won 5) and the Giro, from 1972-1988 (Merckx, 2). The Vuelta's Combined Classification ran from 1970-2018; the record holder being Alejandro Valverde, with 3.

THE GRAND TOURS

Three weeks of epic feats in the world's three most notorious, high-profile cycle races, where teams strain every sinew to propel their star rider to top the podium

The Grand Tours, also known sometimes as the major tours, are three-week races that offer every kind of road-racing challenge, from the clockwork precision of team time trials to epic mountain stages over multiple passes with some of Europe's most dramatic mountain terrain as the arena. Without question, the Tour de France is the biggest of the three races, its history, prestige and level of competition setting it well above the Giro d'Italia and Vuelta a España, and indeed any other race on the calendar. It's the one event that has sporting significance beyond cycling and, as a result, attracts the widest audience. It bills itself as the biggest annual spectator event in global sport, attracting more than 10 million fans to French roadsides year after year, with a viewing audience of hundreds of millions more.

The Tour de France was founded in 1903 by *L'Auto* as a last throw of the dice by its editor-in-chief, Henri Desgrange, to prevent the sports newspaper from going under. Legend has it that one of Desgrange's chief reporters, Géo Lefèvre, sketched out a proposal for the race on the tablecloth of a Paris restaurant, telling his boss that this tour of France would race between some of the nation's biggest cities, attracting not only the best riders of the era but also popular acclaim. While Desgrange wasn't totally convinced, his finance director, Victor Goddet, effectively shrugged as if to say, "What choice do we have?"

GETTING OUT OF THE STARTING BLOCKS

According to the initial announcement, the Tour would take place across the month of June that year. Yet, at a time when multi-day events didn't exist and most potential competitors needed to take time off work to participate, the take-up was negligible. The race was put on ice for a month, then relaunched. The new, shortened version was scheduled for the first 18 days of July, the race comprising six stages with two rest days between each of them: 60 riders signed up.

The omens weren't promising at the start of the opening stage in the Paris suburb of Montgeron. Just a few hundred fans braved the sweltering heat to see the five dozen competitors disappear ❯

Friendships and mutual admiration can be set aside when there are seconds on the line in the world's biggest bike races

Sean 'King' Kelly used his abilities as a sprinter to dominate one-day Classics and also made a big impact on Grand Tours

LEGENDS OF THE SPORT
SEAN KELLY

Kelly's outstanding record in the Classics includes winning four of the five Monuments multiple times, with the exception of the Ronde van Vlaanderen, in which he finished second on three occasions. He won the Points Classification at both the Tour de France and the Vuelta a España twice, but never competed in the Giro. The Irishman is now a GCN+ commentator.

quickly into a billowing cloud of dust at the start of a 467km stage to Lyon. Desgrange was a little dismayed as he made his way back to his office in the centre of the French capital. Yet, almost as soon as the riders were into the countryside, they were greeted with immense enthusiasm by huge crowds.

The Tour was a hit. *L'Auto-Vélo*'s sales soared. Other newspapers took note. After launching the Giro di Lombardia in 1905 and Milano-Sanremo two years later, *La Gazzetta dello Sport* organised the first Giro d'Italia in 1909, and these new events gave the Italian daily a significant edge over its sporting rivals. Although another 26 years passed before the Vuelta a España emerged, that race too was established by a daily paper, *Informaciones*.

Extreme in terms of their length and physical demands, the three races have become central pillars of the cycling calendar, the Tour always standing head and shoulders above its fellow Grand Tours, but all three hugely prized by riders and fans alike. Their sheer length is anomalous in modern-day sport – they are events well outside the norm where the focus is increasingly on shorter, more action-packed contests. However, like cricket's five-day test matches, they offer a spectacle that's not only backed by history and tradition, but provides a longer and often more engrossing narrative, a sporting soap opera that always engages.

❯

GIRO D'ITALIA

*DS **Matt White** on passionate Italian fans
and why the Giro is the most important race of all!*

"I think it all started for me because it was the first Grand Tour
I rode, and because I also lived in Italy; spending my first three
years in Italian teams I saw the passion the Italian teams and Italian
people, as a whole, have for the Giro. That first Grand Tour was the
'98 Giro, when Marco Pantani won. It was the last Grand Tour to
have no rest day because the organisers decided the riders didn't
need one! After that the UCI made it compulsory to have rest days.
It was brutal, but I totally fell in love with the race.

"Going back there as a rider and then as a director, where I've
been involved in some really successful teams, when you're
winning, when you've got the *maglia rosa*, you obviously gain a
different connection to a race in which you haven't had so much
success. I have been part of winning Vuelta teams as well, but I
just have a different feeling around the Giro. The Tour de France
is our sport's global event, and it's obviously a massive global
circus, but the real cycling fans are diluted amongst the people
who are there for the spectacle. At the Giro, on the other hand, the
people watching are true fans of the sport. There's just a different
feeling in Italy in the month of May to being in France in July.

"The food and the wine certainly help, too. Also, some of the best
hotels I go to are at the Giro. You end up in a small hotel, maybe
it's a *pensione* and you might be the only team there. And it's run
by a family and those people are incredibly proud to have you at
their establishment. I've been in some really small hotels up in the
Dolomites when we've had the pink jersey or had a big star on the
team, and you can just sense the buzz and the hype around that,
among the staff, and the family. They can't do enough to help you.
Whereas some of the times on the Tour, when you're staying in yet
another chain hotel, the people there couldn't care less who you
are. At the Giro, it's different."

Matt White

Directeur Sportif at Team
BikeExchange-Jayco, where
he has served in its different
guises for most of his
managerial career since 2012.
As a rider, a stage winner
in numerous top level
stage races, he memorably
outsprinted fellow Australian,
Robbie McEwan, in the 2005
Tour Down Under.

Tom Dumoulin is saluted by Giro fans in 2017 as he prepares to swap his Netherlands national champion's jersey for the maglia rosa

💬 JARGON BUSTER

MAGLIA ROSA

Since 1931, the leader of the general classification has worn the pink jersey – the *maglia rosa* – the colour reflected the colour of the paper on which the Italian sports newspaper *La Gazzetta dello Sport* was printed.

Right: *The Giro's iconic 'Never Ending' trophy lives up to its name… it's extended each year with the winner's name; in 2021 that was the Colombian Egan Bernal*

PRO'S PERSPECTIVE

TOUR DE FRANCE

Ineos Grenadiers' 2018 Tour de France winner
Geraint Thomas *explains what it takes to win the Tour*

"For me a lot of hard work, a lot of years grafting and learning the trade, experience and everything from weight management to the best type of training, to a whole lot of things, leading the team etcetera. If you ask Pogačar he just stepped in and did it straight away, didn't he? So that puts that to bed. But for me it was a whole 12 years accumulating experience. Having no bad luck is a big thing as well. Then at the Tour it's about riding confidently, having a good strong team around you, good morale, and cutting out the outside noise as well. But the main things are being confident and having done the hard work for sure.

"It's not just about being the best, it's about how you race and how you race as a team... We got attacked a lot, a lot of guys were racing aggressively, attacking from a long way out and it would have been easy to sort of panic and just ride too hard, but we stuck together well and didn't panic. I think Nico Portal our DS was key to all that. You need good legs, but I think good heads. The way you ride together makes you almost unbeatable. Just having all those guys riding for me, I know what it's like because I've done that over many years so obviously I really appreciated it and obviously knew how much it meant to them as well.

"When I won the Dauphiné a month before the start of the Tour, that was huge for me because it was my biggest win to that point and it was amazing for the confidence.

"The planning and stuff that the team did was key to it all. We had a lot of extra feeds on the side of the road, for instance, we'd have a guy midway up each of the climbs and at the top handing out bags with four bottles in and some gels and it meant that even the guys who were helping me didn't have to go back to the car. We could just grab them from the side of the road and that made a big difference."

Geraint Thomas

A multiple World Champion, Olympic Champion and world record holder on the track, Thomas has ridden with Team Sky/Ineos since 2010. He's been British champion for both road and time trial, transitioning through one-day Classics to stage race success, culminating in winning a stage on Alpe d'Huez on his way to Tour victory.

Geraint Thomas, the first Welshman to
win the Tour, claimed the yellow jersey
by winning stage 11, then reinforced it by
winning on Alpe d'Huez the next day

 **JARGON
BUSTER**

À BLOC

A French term used to
describe a rider/bunch
racing flat out or full gas.

Left With yellow trim, Team Sky
flank Thomas and enjoy the
traditional flute of champagne on
the processional roll-in to Paris

The Vuelta is a late-season highlight for riders and it's certainly a favourite for fans to get up close to their heroes

INSTANT EXPERT

CONSECUTIVE GRAND TOURS

No rider has ever won all three Grand Tours in one calendar year. But there are three riders who have won all three across two consecutive seasons.

Eddy Merckx 1972/73
Bernard Hinault 1982/83
Chris Froome 2017/18

James Knox is a rising star, with potential talent to match his GC ambitions

PRO'S PERSPECTIVE

VUELTA A ESPAÑA

James Knox from Team Quick-Step-Alpha Vinyl on why the Vuelta is his stand-out Grand Tour

"I've not ridden the Tour de France, and the Giro d'Italia seems a little bit more special as far as fans are concerned, and in terms of the history. Plus I grew up as a rider in Italy, spending a lot of time racing there when from 18-20. Somehow, though, the Vuelta a España is just that little bit more enjoyable to do, particularly because of where it sits now at the end of the season.

"It's a really good way to finish off the year. The Giro takes a lot out of you and, because it's in May, you can feel a bit dead and buried — and you've still got four months of cycling to go. But when you're competing in the Vuelta in August, you're satisfied to be there and, if it goes well, you come out of the season looking forward to the following year.

"There are always arguments about whether the Vuelta organisers get carried away with their hills, mountains and punchy finishes, but they suit me, so I'm not going to complain. As a counterpoint to that, the Giro has a lot of really long days, for which I know there are some arguments because those huge stages are one of the race's traditions, but as a rider, if you're having a hard time and you see that there are another 220-230km still to come, well, you tend to dread it. And there's less of that in the Vuelta.

"Then there's the weather, which really suits me. Some of the guys ride well in the miserable weather, but I think almost everyone prefers it when it's sunny. That said, you do get some days in the Vuelta when it's simply too hot. Talking about the weather — it's one of those things you can complain about all the time: it's either too cold at the Giro, or too hot at the Vuelta. But for me personally, give me the heat every time."

James Knox

Young British rider James is a World Tour GC contender, racking up top 15 placings in the Vuelta and the Giro, as well as top-10 positions in the UAE Tour and Tirreno-Adriatico.

With the peloton strung out, at pace, riders are forgiven for not taking in the amazing scenery, as fans have the luxury of doing

Primož Roglič delighted in winning the 2022 edition of Paris-Nice, joining such luminaries as Sean Kelly, winner of seven consecutive editions in the 1980s

STAT ATTACK!

DAUPHINÉ-TOUR DOUBLE

Eleven riders have achieved the Critérium du Dauphiné and Tour de France double:

Louison **Bobet** (1955)
Jacques **Anquetil** (1963)
Eddy **Merckx** (1971)
Luis **Ocaña** (1973)
Bernard **Thévenet** (1975)
Bernard **Hinault** (1979, 1981)
Miguel **Indurain** (1995)
Lance **Armstrong***
(2002, 2003)
Bradley **Wiggins** (2012)
Chris **Froome**
(2013, 2015 & 2016)
Geraint **Thomas** (2018)

SUISSE/TOUR DOUBLE

Only three riders have won the Tour de Suisse and the Tour de France in the same year:

Eddy **Merckx** (1974)
Lance **Armstrong*** (2001)
Egan **Bernal** (2019)

* Armstrong's record expunged

LEADING STAGE RACES

These 'local' races are every fan's dream as the peloton sweeps past front door or kids' school alike, while teams vie to stake their claim to UCI points and glory

MEN'S

PARIS-NICE

'The Race to the Sun' takes place in early March and travels from the outskirts of Paris, still in the embrace of winter, to the Côte d'Azur, where spring is well on its way. Established in 1933, the prestigious eight-day event usually goes right down to the wire, the overall result in doubt until the riders sweep down the Col d'Eze above Nice at the end of the final stage.

TIRRENO-ADRIATICO

First run in 1966, the seven-day stage race from Italy's Tyrrhenian coast to the Adriatic is usually the race of choice for riders with Milano-Sanremo in their sights. Mixing spectacularly steep hill-top finishes with rolling stages, its winner rides away with one of the most impressive trophies in sport in the shape of a huge trident.

TOUR DE ROMANDIE

Located in the French-speaking western part of Switzerland, the race extends to six days and brings together riders who are ❯

Tirreno-Adriatico's impressive trident trophy reflects the race's nautical nature

The Giro d'Italia Donne is the toughest of the Women's WorldTour stage races – where Dutch riders including Marianne Vos are dominant

Cycling is the only sport where the household names come right past your... household

LEGENDS OF THE SPORT
MARIANNE VOS

By 2021 peerless Vos had won an incredible **30 stages** of the **Giro d'Italia Donne**. The rider next on the list isn't even close; that's Petra Rossner, the German rider with 17 stage wins. Vos had passed her record way back in 2014 and has just been adding to it ever since. The breadth of riders she's been beating over the course of 14 years is also astonishing; there are 19 different riders she has beaten into second place. The worst afflicted? Giorgia Bronzini, who Vos got the better of on four different stages across three different editions.

"The Giro d'Italia Donne is the one major stage race that has survived from the vibrant '80s"

targeting the Grand Tours. Some use it as the final stepping stone to the Giro d'Italia, others as a first test on the road to the Tour de France. Its late-April date means the weather can be challenging.

CRITÉRIUM DU DAUPHINÉ

Set up in 1947 by the *Dauphiné Libéré* newspaper in the southern French Alps, it was taken over by Tour organisers ASO in 2010 and has since spread its reach beyond that region. Held over a week in early June, it's a key marker of pre-Tour form and concludes with three back-to-back mountain stages.

TOUR DE SUISSE

Founded in 1933, it is the only 10-day stage race on the WorldTour calendar. Like the Dauphiné, it's ostensibly used to fine-tune form before the Tour de France. With two time trials, a good number of sprint stages and a handful of days in the mountains, there's plenty of terrain for every type of rider to shine.

WOMEN'S GIRO D'ITALIA DONNE

Established in 1988, it is the one major stage race on the calendar that has survived from what was then a very vibrant stage racing scene. Ten days long, it tends to focus on one part of Italy each year, and more often than not that is in the north, which is the heartland of the country's cycling heritage.

TOUR DE FRANCE FEMMES

Regarded by some as a relaunched version of the Tour de France that ran between 1984 and 1993, but promoted by organisers ASO as a completely new race with Zwift sponsoring, its inaugural 2022 edition was scheduled to run from Paris to the Vosges Mountains over eight days.

VUELTA A BURGOS FEMININAS

Four stages of flat, hilly and mountainous terrain in the Spanish province of Burgos makes for an exciting, absorbing race that, in 2021 at any rate, favoured the peloton's strongest hill climbers, Anna van der Breggen and Annemiek van Vleuten.

RIDE LONDON CLASSIQUE

Now upgraded to two stages in undulating (not flat) Essex, with a sprint dash to the finish line on London's Victoria Embankment on the third day, this race requires strength and speed.   ❯

Rain or shine, the Spring Classics deliver thrills and spills and heroic racing performances

RACE CLASSIFICATON NUMBERING EXPLAINED

The UCI's Race Classification system may not be exactly pretty but it's useful for quickly understanding the nature and level of each race

Each race code is made of two or three parts. The first is a number, either 1 or 2, where 1 denotes a single-day race, and 2 denotes a multi-day stage race.

The second part of the code describes the race's ranking. The highest designation is 'UWT' or 'WWT' – in which WorldTeams / Women's WorldTeams must participate, and Pro Continental teams can, with a WildCard entry. Then it's 'Pro', open to a maximum of 70% WorldTeams, all Pro Continental teams, Continental teams from the country the race is organised in and a maximum of two others, and National teams from the country the race is organised in.

The next designation down is '1', for a maximum of 50% WorldTeams, plus Pro Continental, Continental and National teams. The lowest designation is '2': open to Pro Continental teams from the country the race is organised in (and two from other countries), Continental, National, Regional and Club teams.

Some races have a third classification index, where the letter 'U' denotes an Under-23 race, or 'NCup' specifies a Nations Cup race involving national teams or 'mixed teams'.

So, a 1.2 race would be a one-day race (hence the "1.") featuring a range of teams from lower down the hierarchy (hence the ".2") , such as the Belgian Grote Prijs Rik Van Looy race in July, while a 2.WWT race would be a multi-day stage race (hence the "2.") in the Women's WorldTour (WWT), such as Itzulia Women (in the Basque country, in May), and a top-level stage race in the men's WorldTour – such as the Tour de France – has a 2.UWT designation.

Mathieu van der Poel re he's just won a 1.UWT r 2019's Amstel Gold

WHY I LOVE THE CLASSICS
Mads Pedersen

"The Classics are great for me because I'm not skinny enough to do the Grand Tours. I think most kids dream about the Tour, and have it as our goal, then quickly find out that we're too heavy to go for the GC and then we have to find a plan B. That's the Classics. They're special races where you have to take everything into account – hoping your bike and materials will last the super-long course, racing over cobblestones on long days. Most of the time the weather is bad, too, adding another element to them."

THE CLASSICS

These intense injections of blood, sweat and tears are masterclasses in thrills and spills for fans and riders, their unpredictability one of their winning ingredients

The Classics are cycling's blockbusters; one-day races that offer a gripping mix of history, tradition, brutality and iconic locations, and with barely a lull in the action throughout. That said, the only trait the Classics really share is their duration. Some are cobbled, others hilly, some are both. There's also a new fad for gravel and dirt. The overall essence is of unpredictability. These are races where riders can't let their attention wander for an instant – and fans shouldn't either.

HOW THEY ALL STARTED

The Classics have their roots in the late 19th century. The first to see the light of day was Liège-Bastogne-Liège, which was first run in 1892. However, it was Paris-Roubaix, founded four years later, that first captured the public's attention and enthusiasm. It was set up by two textile magnates in the industrial city in France's north-east to promote the opening of the city's velodrome. The pair hoped that running a race from Paris to Roubaix would raise the profile of the new track they'd funded, as well as fill a gap in the programme of events taking place in the velodrome that day. However, it was the road race won by Germany's Josef Fischer that stole the show and, very quickly, became the event that put Paris-Roubaix firmly on the cycling map.

That same year, the first edition of Paris-Tours took place. Together with Paris-Roubaix and Bordeaux-Paris, first run in 1891 and at 560 kilometres the longest of them all, these three races were the basis of what gradually became the Classics. In the first decade of the 20th century, they were joined by the Giro di Lombardia, rebranded Il Lombardia in recent years, and its sister event Milano-Sanremo. The first edition of the Ronde van Vlaanderen took place in May 1913, this too organised by a newspaper, *Sportswereld*, who soon moved it to the weekend before Paris-Roubaix, making the two events the fulcrum for the Northern Classics. These races are mainly run on the cobbles and bergs of the Flemish Ardennes and include Het Nieuwsblad (formerly Het Volk), Kuurne-Brussel-Kuurne,

"It was Paris-Roubaix that first captured the public's attention and enthusiasm"

Friends are made and lost in the peloton as favours are swapped and banked across the seasons

OMLOOP HET NIEUWSBLAD
The season's first major race in Northern Europe

MILANO-TORINO
The oldest classic; until recently raced in Autumn

MILANO-SANREMO MONUMENT
'La Primavera', first of the Monuments

GENT-WEVELGEM
Race 2 of 'Flanders Week' on Belgian cobbles

RONDE VAN VLAANDEREN
MONUMENT 'De Ronde' is Belgium's biggest race

PARIS-ROUBAIX MONUMENT
'The Hell of the North'; iconic cobbled Classic

LA FLÈCHE WALLONNE
Mid-week Ardennes classic with the Mur de Huy

GIRO DELL'EMILIA
Climbing-focused circuit-based Classic, from 1909

IL LOMBARDIA MONUMENT
'The Race of the Falling Leaves' and fifth Monument

FEBRUARY   **MARCH**   **APRIL**   **OCTOBER**

KUURNE-BRUSSEL-KUURNE
The Sunday of the opening Classics weekend

GP E3 HARELBEKE
Cobbled classic, now called E3 Saxo Bank

DWARS DOOR VLAANDEREN
Exciting mid-week build-up to De Ronde

GP SCHELDEPRIJS
The oldest Belgian race now nips into Holland

AMSTEL GOLD RACE
Highlights that The Netherlands does have hills!

LIÈGE-BASTOGNE-LIÈGE MONUMENT
The oldest and arguably toughest Monument

GRAN PIEMONTE
Semi-classic, mid-week preparation for Il Lombardia

PARIS-TOURS
Once the Sprinters' Classic, now featuring dirt roads

Women's and men's Classics seasons open with Belgium's Omloop Het Nieuwsblad in late February

INSTANT EXPERT

CLASSIC OR MONUMENT?

The five biggest and most prestigious one-day Classics are the Monument Classics: **Milano-Sanremo**, **Ronde van Vlaanderen**, **Paris-Roubaix**, **Liège-Bastogne-Liège** and **Il Lombardia**.

"The Classics gained a boost with the establishment of the Colombo-Desgrange Challenge"

GP E3 Harelbeke, Gent-Wevelgem and Dwars door Vlaanderen. Following the Second World War, the Classics gained a substantial boost with the establishment of the Colombo-Desgrange Challenge. First organised in 1948 by four newspapers – *L'Équipe*, *Het Nieuwsblad-Sportswereld*, *La Gazzetta dello Sport* and *Les Sports* – this season-long series was designed to encourage the leading riders to compete in the major events run by each of these newspaper groups. That year, it included the Tour de France and the Giro d'Italia, Paris-Roubaix, Milano-Sanremo, Il Lombardia, Flèche Wallonne, Paris-Brussels and Paris-Tours. Subsequently, further races were added, notably Liège-Bastogne-Liège (1951) and the Vuelta a España (1958). Through various new manifestations of the Colombo-Desgrange series, most of these races have found their place on the calendar, supplemented by a few more recent additions, among them GP E3 (1958), the Amstel Gold Race (1966) and Strade Bianche (2007). ❯

In his breakthrough year, 2022, Eritrea's Biniam Girmay won Gent-Wevelgem and set about attacking the Giro d'Italia

INSTANT EXPERT

WHAT'S A SEMI-CLASSIC?

There are a number of other one-day races of significance throughout the cycling season, considered by some (often the race organisers) to be classics, more often as 'semi-classics', and occasionally refered to as 'emerging classics'. They include Kuurne-Brussel-Kuurne (men only), Strade Bianche (both), Trofeo Alfredo Binda (women only), Dwars door Vlaanderen, Scheldeprijs, De Brabantse Pijl (all both), Tro Bro Léon (men only), Bretagne Classic (both), Clásica San Sebastian, Giro dell'Emilia and Gran Piemonte (men only).

Winning Amstel Gold Race Ladies is thirsty work, as Marta Cavalli discovered in 2022

GROUPS OF CLASSICS

Italian Spring Classics: the big one, Milano-Samremo, recently joined by Milano-Torino, and loosely including Strade Bianche.

The Cobbled Classics: E3 Harelbeke, Gent-Wevelgem, Ronde van Vlaanderen, Paris-Roubaix and a number of other smaller races.

The Ardennes Classics ('Ardennes Week'): the back-to-back thrillers, Amstel Gold Race; La Flèche Wallonne, Liège-Bastogne-Liège. The Cobbled Classics and the Ardennes Classics together are known as the **Northern Classics.**

All of the above loosely make up the **Spring Classics.**

The Summer Classics (overshadowed by the Grand Tours) include Clásica de San Sebastián in Spain, Bretagne Classic in France and two one-day races in Canada, the GP de Québec and GP de Montréal, themselves known as The Laurentian Classics, after the Saint Lawrence River.

Autumn Classics: Paris–Brussels (now known as the Brussels Cycling Classic and only run on Belgian territory), Paris-Tours (in France!), and three Italian races, with the Giro dell'Emilia and the Gran Piemonte being the build up to Il Lombardia.

IMPORTANT 'CLASSICS'

What defines a Classic is the subject of debate, but here are the big one-day races outside of the Monuments...

OMLOOP HET NIEUWSBLAD *MEN'S & WOMEN'S*

With the men's race first held in 1945, this season-opener features many of the cobbles and bergs that will define the bigger races. It's highly prestigious for the women's peloton, dating from 2006.

MILANO-TORINO

The oldest one-day race on the calendar, from 1876, it has recently reinvented itself by moving from autumn to spring ahead of Milano-Sanremo and introducing a flat, sprinter-friendly parcours.

GP E3 HARELBEKE

The 'mini Ronde van Vlaanderen' opens Flemish week and, while shorter, uses many of the same roads and hills as 'De Ronde'. Belgium's Tom Boonen holds the record with five wins.

GENT-WEVELGEM *MEN'S & WOMEN'S*

Regularly over 250km for the men this race (born 1934) often sees a chase between escapees and the bunch after the final ascent of the Kemmelberg. Multiple winners include Boonen, Eddy Merckx and Kirsten Wild, with the women's race having begun in 2012.

AMSTEL GOLD RACE *MEN'S & WOMEN'S*

Although geographically impossible, this Dutch race is the first of the Ardennes classics. Raced in the hilly Limburg region its Cauberg climb is often decisive. The men's race dates from 1966 and the women's 2001 (despite a hefty hiatus, 2003-2017).

LA FLÈCHE WALLONNE *MEN'S & WOMEN'S*

Dating from 1936, the race is nowadays always decided on the final ascent of the fearsome Mur de Huy. The women's race dates from 1998; Anna van der Breggan holds the record with seven wins, achieved in consecutive seasons between 2015 and 2021.

PARIS-TOURS

Dating back to 1896, this race of over 250km gained a reputation as a 'sprinter's classic' due to the lack of big hills and long finishing straight on the Avenue de Grammont. It has lost some of its historic stature, and since 2019 has taken place the day after Il Lombardia, incorporating sectors of the wine region's dirt roads since 2018. ❯

MONUMENT

MILANO-SANREMO

Est. 1907

Revered by Italians for its complexity and its thrilling build up, Milano-Sanremo often goes right to the wire

Imagine trying to make this pitch in the modern era: "It'll be a 300-kilometre-plus race, starting in one of Europe's great cities and finishing in a fading seaside resort, with one categorised climb at the mid-point, but almost always decided by what happens on a small hill that tops out less than half-a-dozen kilometres from the finish." It made sense when it was first run in 1907, when Sanremo was one of Europe's most glamorous resorts. But today?

Oddly, without trying too hard to adapt to the changing face of bike racing and sport, 'La Primavera' has remained vibrant and thrilling. Organisers RCS have stuck essentially to the original script, making just minor tweaks to toughen up the finale on the Ligurian coast, the most significant of these being the addition of ❯

Wout van Aert covers Julian Alaphilippe's attack on the Poggio, Milano-Sanremo's final climb

"*La Primavera has remained vibrant and thrilling... with just minor tweaks to toughen up the finale on the Ligurian coast*"

the climbs of the Poggio in 1960 and the Cipressa in 1982. In doing so, they have found an intriguing balance between pure bunch sprinters and *puncheurs*.

A THRILLER OF A RACE

While some dismiss it as a race where nothing much happens for seven hours, it's much more complex than that, particularly for Italian riders and fans, who revere it. Former *La Gazzetta dello Sport* journalist, Marco Pastonesi, described it as building up like a thriller. It starts early in the morning when Milan is cold and dank, crossing the misty Piemonte plains to reach its major climbing test, the Passo del Turchino. Here, in 1947, Fausto Coppi went clear on his own, his attack initiating a staggering 150km solo raid that ended with the legendary Italian finishing 14 minutes clear of runner-up Lucien Teisseire.

From the tunnel at the top of the Turchino, the riders emerge into bright sunlight and the second and more temperate coastal section of the race, marking the change from winter to spring. The race is spectacular as it hugs the Mediterranean, gliding through resorts that are just starting to wake from winter, bobbing over the dramatic headlands of the Capo Mele, Capo Cervo and Capo Berta, the pace and intensity rising all the time.

At San Lorenzo al Mare, the route veers inland and up, over the Cipressa, the harder of the two final climbs, stringing the bunch out. Less than 10km later, the riders kick up for the final time on the Poggio di Sanremo. Here, on gentle slopes that are tackled at tremendous velocity, the balance starts to tip one way or the other. Can the *puncheurs* deliver that extra burst of speed that will give them the vital few seconds they need down the twisting descent into Sanremo, or will the sprinters' teams keep them within their grasp, bringing what remains of the bunch back together as it flies into Sanremo, the verdict unclear right to the very last?

STAT ATTACK!

MILANO-SANREMO *3 biggest winning margins*

YEAR	WINNER	RUNNER-UP	MARGIN
1910	Eugène **Christophe**	Giovanni **Cocchi**	1:01:00
1946	Fausto **Coppi**	Lucien **Teisseire**	14:00
1918	Gaetano **Belloni**	Costante **Girardengo**	13:00

PRO'S PERSPECTIVE

WHY SANREMO?
Filippo Ganna

"I think it's one of the most important races we have in Italy after the Giro. Even though it has a reputation for no climbs and nothing special in the first part, you still see all the big names on the start line. It has something special... It's quite something to stand in Milan and think that, in seven hours, you'll be in Sanremo and when you get there you might be transformed into a big cycling star. Sanremo can be a strange race because you can reach the Poggio, the decisive climb, with fantastic legs and after two corners you can be done — and you don't know why! You need to be in really, really good shape because it affects your body and your power in an unusual way."

💬 **JARGON BUSTER**

PUNCHEUR

A rider with explosive power who tends to make the most of that attribute on short but steep climbs. Julian Alaphilippe and Mathieu van der Poel are good examples of this breed.

The attrition over La Primavera's long distance means teams need to protect their leaders for the final showdown

Jasper Stuyven's late attack on the 2021 edition stuck, as the chasing pack couldn't reel him back in

"Perhaps more than any other race on the calendar, the Ronde van Vlaanderen encapsulates the region and the people who live there"

The steep, cobbled Kapelmuur is a regular feature of the Ronde van Vlaanderen, softening riders up before the finale

MONUMENT

RONDE VAN VLAANDEREN

Est. 1913

History and cycle sport combine in this exacting tour of Flemish monuments, which includes 125km of cobbles

The Ronde van Vlaanderen (the Tour of Flanders) was created by *Sportswereld* journalists Karel Van Wijnendaele and Leon Van den Haute in 1913, the race designed not only to boost the circulation of that title but also assert the Flemish language, culture and rights in Belgium, where French was at that time predominant. The route of the inaugural race started and finished in Gent, passing through as many Flemish cities as possible on its 330km loop. While the route has changed substantially over the last century, Flanders retains that founding sense of importance for Belgium's Dutch-speaking population. As much as any other race on the calendar, it encapsulates the region and the people who live there, drawing as many as one-in-five of the Flemish population onto the roadside.

The race's characteristic features are its climbs, or bergs, and the long sections of cobbled roads. However, the first races didn't venture into the steeply undulating Flemish Ardennes. Even ❯

The Flemish bergs make De Ronde, and make or break reputations

until the early 1970s, there were no more than half a dozen on the route, these sought out by Van Wijnendaele as councils gradually resurfaced the cobbled roads that provided the Ronde's defining test. During the 1970s and 1980s, this steady drift towards the hills increased dramatically, introducing the Bosberg, the Oude Kwaremont, the fearsomely steep cobbles of the Koppenberg, the Kapelmuur at Geraardsbergen and the Paterberg. Since the turn of the century the race has featured as many as 19 climbs packed into 250-odd kilometres of racing, more than half of them cobbled and now preserved as national monuments.

UPDATING FOR THE 21ST CENTURY

In 2012, the sheer volume of race traffic as fans tracked the action from place to place, triggered a controversial restructure of the course that included a finishing circuit featuring the cobbled ascents of the Oude Kwaremont, Paterberg and Koppenberg. It also enabled the organisers, Flanders Classics, to boost the number of VIP areas and, thus, its revenue. Although the loss of the iconic Kapelmuur was widely condemned for some years, the revamped course based on the finishing town of Oudenaarde, home to the Tour of Flanders Centre, has proved a success. The essence of Flanders has been maintained, the route still favouring those with local knowledge, riders who know where they need to be at particular points in the race and how it is likely to unfold.

Ronde van Vlaanderen voor Vrouwen (The Tour of Flanders for Women) was established in 2004 (with nine climbs over 94km, won by Russia's Zulfiya Zabirova from Germany's Trixi Worrack) had a rebrand in 2021, the organisers renaming it the Ronde van Vlaanderen (Tour of Flanders) and differentiating the two Classics by categorising them as 'Elite Women' and 'Elite Men'. That 2021 edition was won by The Netherlands' Annemiek van Vleuten (from Germany's Lisa Brennauer), who finished alone at the end of a 152km race that featured 13 classified climbs.   ⟩

INSTANT EXPERT

HET NIEUWSBLAD AND FLANDERS DOUBLE

No male rider has ever won Het Nieuwsblad and the Ronde van Vlaanderen in the same year. The thinking being that if you're fit enough early in the season to win Het Nieuwsblad, you've peaked too early and you'll never be able to hold your form until De Ronde. One female rider has managed it though, Lizzie Deignan in 2016.

PRO'S PERSPECTIVE

REAL RACING
Sylvain Chavanel

"I used to love racing on those cobbles where everything depended on your positioning. That was real racing, everything you learnt in cycling school could be found at the Ronde van Vlaanderen. I was spellbound by the atmosphere... I quickly realised this was a race like no other."

RONDE VAN VLAANDEREN *Top 3 winning margins*

YEAR	WINNER	RUNNER-UP	MARGIN
1919	Henri **Van Lerberghe**	Leon **Buysse**	14:00
1930	Frans **Bonduel**	Aimé **Dossche**	9:15
1922	Léon **Devos**	Jean **Brunier**	7:40

Pre-race teams presentations have rockstar status at Ronde van Vlaanderen. It's another unique part of the fan's experience in pro cycling

Sylvain Chavanel won the Dwars Door Vlaanderen, but the Ronde van Vlaanderen victory eluded him... in ten attempts his highest position was 2nd, in 2011

PRO'S PERSPECTIVE

I LOVE DE RONDE!

Jasper Stuyven

"Why do I love the Ronde van Vlaanderen? Everyone knows exactly how the final needs to be ridden and where the key points are. It's exciting to have all the fans at the side of the road. Having the public all around you is what makes Flanders such an exciting day, a race that I think everyone looks forward to."

MONUMENT

PARIS-ROUBAIX

Est. 1896

This is the Classic that attracts vast numbers, all mesmerised by the brutal mix of pavé and climate

Known as 'The Queen of the Classics' and 'The Hell of the North', Paris-Roubaix is the Classic that transcends bike racing. The chaotic and magnificent action that takes place on its 50 or so kilometres of cobbled pavé attracts a broader audience of sports fans, mesmerised by what is undoubtedly road racing's most barbaric challenge.

Its hellish reputation stems from the post-war edition of 1919. Its winner, Frenchman Henri Pélissier, undertook a reconnaissance of the route that he described unforgettably in *L'Auto*: "We enter into the centre of the battlefield. There's not a tree, everything is flattened! Not a square metre that has not been hurled upside down. There's one shell hole after another. The only things that stand out in this churned earth are the crosses with their ribbons in blue, white and red. It is hell!"

MODERNISING FOR POSTERITY

In the first half of the 20th century, almost all the roads between Paris and Roubaix were laid with cobbles – granite setts, to be more precise, square-ish blocks put down originally in uniform rows, their surface and the gaps between them distorted over time by traffic and the elements. There were hills, too, the most significant of them being the long drag out of Doullens, which often split the field.

Following the Second World War, as local councils pushed towards modernisation by improving transport links, the amount of pavé diminished radically, reaching a nadir in the mid-'60s, when there were only two dozen kilometres along a route that wasn't far short of 300km in length. Yet, coinciding with the move of the start from Paris to first Chantilly and, in 1977, to current departure point of Compiègne, ASO focused on digging up new sections of   **›**

"Riders and fans are in thrall to what is undoubtedly road racing's most barbaric challenge"

2021: Mathieu van der Poel battles through the elements in the first rainy 'Roubaix' in 20 years

This is what a Monument means: Italy's Sonny Colbrelli shows the emotion of winning in the Roubaix velodrome, having outsprinted Florian Vermeersch and Mathieu van der Poel

FREEZE FRAME

In 2021 Trek-Segafredo's Lizzie Deignan won the first Paris-Roubaix Femmes after making an audacious breakaway, riding solo for 80 of the 115.6km and across all 17 cobbled section — and being chased down by the mighty Marianne Vos. With neither racing in 2022 it was Deignan's teammate Elisa Longo Borghini who solo'd to the win!

ROUBAIX DEBUT WINNERS

In 2021 Italy's Sonny Colbrelli was the first male rider to win Paris-Roubaix on his debut since Germain Derycke in 1953. Lizzie Deignan won her – and *the* – first Paris-Roubaix Femmes in the same year.

> **"The unprecedented challenge that Roubaix sets the racers continues right to the finish"**

INSTANT EXPERT

PRAY FOR RAIN!

At Paris-Roubaix, fans pray for rain. Why? Because in the dry it's a brutal series of tough cobbled sections ready to break riders and bikes alike. Paris-Roubaix in the wet takes the danger and unpredictablity up another two or three notches, as the tops of the cobbles become coatde with slippery mud and the gaps between them, 'chicken nests' as some French call them, fill with water and mud, making them even harder to judge.

pavé, literally in many cases, where old roads had become lost in fields or covered with decades of mud and muck. The sectors at Arenberg, Carrefour de l'Arbre and Mons-en-Pévèle, the only three that are ranked as five-star in terms of degree of difficulty, were all added to the race during this period.

The race now features around 55km of pavé, the first at Troisvilles at around the 100km mark, the last a short stretch in Roubaix itself just before reaching the velodrome. Like the cobbles in the Flemish Ardennes, the pavé, once seen as highlighting a lack of development in the north, are now viewed as emblematic of the region and have protection orders on them. They're restored and maintained by Les Amis de Roubaix, a group comprising thousands of volunteers dedicated to preserving the roads that have always been the essence of the race.

IT AIN'T OVER UNTIL IT'S OVER

The unprecedented challenge that Roubaix sets the racers continues right to the finish, which still takes place at an outdoor velodrome. This track isn't the original constructed in the late 19th century, but was built in 1936 and first hosted the finish of Roubaix seven years later. Having the finale here adds to the race's mystique and unique nature, four-time winner Tom Boonen calling it, "The most beautiful 250m in the world". It's actually twice that, but probably doesn't feel that way when riders are circling it, thousands of fans yelling in the grandstands, victory depending not only on strength, but also on their sprint on the banked track. In 2021, Lizzie Deignan won the first Paris-Roubaix Femmes, where the wet and difficult conditions encouraged her to make an attack going into the first of 17 sections of cobbles, more than 80km out from the finish. ❯

PARIS-ROUBAIX *3 biggest winning margins*

YEAR	WINNER	RUNNER-UP	MARGIN
1898	Maurice **Garin**	Auguste **Stéphane**	28:00
1901	Lucien **Lesna**	Ambroise **Garin**	26:00
1896	Josef **Fischer**	Charles **Meyer**	25:00

PRO'S PERSPECTIVE

PARIS-ROUBAIX

*Here's how DS **Dirk Demol** remembers his
'Hell of the North' win in 1998*

"First of all, you either love the race or you hate it. People often say that you need luck to win Roubaix, but what I always say is that what you don't need is bad luck. If you can get through the race without any bad luck, then you can go a long way. You need to have the legs too, of course. When you get to the end you do need luck on your side, and that was definitely the case with my victory. I got into the early breakaway, 230km out, and I thought, 'OK, my DS will be happy because I've already done part of my job'. I was sure the favourites would reel us in eventually, but I believe it's still the only breakaway that made it to the finish... and I won that day despite being a complete outsider.

"On the other hand, when you go into the race with a clear leader – I was the DS when Tom Boonen won with QuickStep and also the year Fabian Cancellara won – you just have to make sure that everything is well set up, everything is well organised, that on every cobbled section you have people who can provide service to the riders, like bottles, or wheels.

"Having the right technique makes a difference. Essentially it comes down to how you race over cobbles. You need speed so that you almost float over the cobbles. When many of the riders reach a section of cobbles they're too cramped, too tense on their bike. I was lucky because in my first years as a professional, I was a teammate of 'Monsieur Paris-Roubaix', Roger De Vlaeminck, and when we did the recon, he told me, 'Listen, you have to give your bike some freedom'. That might sound a bit strange, because while you have to hold your handlebars firmly, you need to do it without clenching your hands. If you grip too tightly, your arms will hurt like hell at halfway. This technique is actually about giving your bike some freedom."

Dirk Demol

After riding for Team ADR in the 1980s and '90s, Belgian Demol was Sporting Director for Team Katusha-Alpecin and, latterly, at the Israel Cycling Academy. Based on his life-changing experience as a rider, he specialises in the Spring Classics.

Dirk Demol's feat of winning Paris-Roubaix from a successful breakaway is super rare!

Left In 2005 Belgium's Tom Boonen rode to the first of his four Paris-Roubaix victories, after the first of his three De Ronde wins, and on his way to becoming World Champion!

Fans know the double-digits ascent of the Côte de Saint Roch will slow and bunch the peloton, giving them great views of the stars

In the sunny 2022 Liège, it was Remco Evenepoel making history, winning solo on his debut to bring home an all-Belgian podium

MONUMENT
LIÈGE-BASTOGNE-LIÈGE
Est. 1892

Snow, hail and ice can all hit the toughest – and oldest – Monument, 'La Doyenne', raced in the Ardennes

Inspired by the astonishing success of 1,200km Paris-Brest-Paris of 1891, the oldest of the Monuments was originally planned as an epic 845km race from Liège to Paris and back. However, the Liège Cyclists' Union that was behind it had to scale back its ambitions and opt for a race of less than a third of that length, still starting and finishing in Liège but with the small town of Bastogne chosen as the halfway point because there was a direct train link there. This allowed for a check point that the riders had to pass through.

Although it remained an almost permanent fixture on the racing calendar, Liège essentially remained a national event overshadowed by its sister race, La Flèche Wallonne, until the 1950s when it became part of the Colombo-Desgrange ›

STAT ATTACK!
LA DOYENNE'S HONOUR ROLL

Eddy Merckx holds the record for the most victories at 'La Doyenne', with five; three of them consecutively, 1971-3. Italy's Moreno Argentin (1980s) and Spain's Alejandro Valverde (2000s) each have four wins.

Eight other Belgians have multiple victories – but spare a thought for Raymond Impanis, winner of De Ronde, Paris-Roubaix and Gent-Wevelgem, who finished second at Liege three times in the 1950s, but never won.

The huge, beguiling Ardennes forest can offer riders respite or renewed terror

Annemiek van Vleuten took her second Liège win in 2022 with a super solo attack

Challenge. This proved the making of it, its relentlessly undulating, and demanding, route favouring the best riders in the sport. Eddy Merckx won it a record five times, the punchy Moreno Argentin and Alejandro Valverde four each. Its reputation as the toughest of the lot was sealed in 1980, when snow and intense cold saw off most of the field. With 80km remaining, Bernard Hinault went to the front of the lead group to raise the pace. When the Frenchman looked back to see who was with him, he found he was alone, finishing more than nine minutes clear of runner-up, Hennie Kuiper, as just 21 hardy competitors finished.

"Its reputation was sealed in 1980, when snow and intense cold saw off most of the field"

A MODERN TEST OF THE STRONG ALL-ROUNDER

Liège is a race of two parts, the outward leg to Bastogne winding through the dense and sometimes forbidding Ardennes forest. At the turn, the route climbs out of the steep-sided valleys onto exposed plateaux, then hurtles back down again. The most renowned of its hills is the Côte de Wanne, the first key point for the favourites to show they're in the game; the short, steep ramp of the Côte de Stockeu, where Merckx would test his rivals; the Côte de la Redoute, climbs steeply out of 2011 winner Philippe Gilbert's home town of Remouchamps; and the more recent addition of the Côte de la Roche-aux-Faucons, which carries the riders up to the outskirts of Liège. Between 1992 and 2018, the race finished on a long drag through the city's industrial suburb of Ans. Since then, it has returned to the centre of Liège, tipping the balance slightly away from the peloton's best climbers and a little more towards those with all-round strengths.

First run in 2017, Liège-Bastogne-Liège Femmes is around half the distance of the men's event, starting in Bastogne and heading north to finish in Liège. Five of the first six editions were won by Dutch riders with only Britain's Lizzie Deignan bucking the trend. ❯

LEGENDS OF THE SPORT
ALEJANDRO VALVERDE

'El Bala' (The Bullet) became the grandfather of the WorldTour peloton, racing in 2022 at the age of 42. His success has spanned two decades with 11 years between his first and latest Liège-Bastogne-Liège victories (2006 and 2017). He also won La Flèche Wallonne in the same years. There are six years between the first and most recent of his four Vuelta a España points classifications wins (2012 and 2018), seven years between Tour de France stages (2005 and 2012) and 14 years spanning his Volta a la Comunitat Valenciana titles (2004, 2007, 2018).

STAT ATTACK!

LIÈGE-BASTOGNE-LIÈGE *Top 3 winning margins*

YEAR	WINNER	RUNNER-UP	MARGIN
1893	Léon **Houa**	Michel **Borisowski**	30:00
1892	Léon **Houa**	Léon **Lhoest**	22:00
1928	Ernest **Mottard**	Maurits **Raes**	12:00

MONUMENT

IL LOMBARDIA

Est. 1905

'The Race of the Falling Leaves' is the final Monument of the year, and a late season test for the peloton's climbers

Founded in 1905 by *La Gazzetta dello Sport*, Il Lombardia, as it has recently been rebranded (originally the Giro di Lombardia), has undergone a significant revamp of its route. It began as a predominantly flat race around Lombardy with the start and finish in Milan, but has gradually edged northwards into the hills around Lake Como and the cities of Bergamo and Como, becoming the Monument that best suits the peloton's pure climbers.

This shift began in 1919 with the introduction of the climb to the Madonna del Ghisallo chapel in Magreglio, sitting high on the promontory that juts northwards into Lake Como. The great Italian climber Costante Girardengo won that edition, his success heralding a golden age for Italian cycling that saw the emergence of Alfredo Binda, Gino Bartali and Fausto Coppi. From 1937, the finish was switched to the newly built Vigorelli indoor velodrome in Milan, which would become one of the sport's legendary venues partly due to its long association with 'the autumn criterium', as Il Lombardia had initially been dubbed by its organisers.

INNOVATION THE KEY TO SUCCESS

As with Paris-Roubaix and Ronde van Vlaanderen, Lombardia's organisers also had to respond to post-war modernisation that ❯

STAT ATTACK!

IL LOMBARDIA *3 biggest winning margins*

YEAR	WINNER	RUNNER-UP	MARGIN
1905	Giovanni **Gerbi**	Giovanni **Rossignoli**	40:11
1926	Alfredo **Binda**	Antonio **Negrini**	29:40
1923	Giovanni **Brunero**	Pietro **Linari**	18:37

*Tadej Pogačar outgunned Bergamo-born
Fausto Masnada in the 2021 edition as the
Slovenian secured his second Monument*

"The Muro di Sormano details with agonising precision each individual metre of elevation gained"

encompassed the resurfacing of dirt roads, including the one over the Ghisallo pass, which was significant in more than 80 riders contesting the 1959 edition. Race director Vincenzo Torriani's solution was the introduction of the Muro di Sormano climb — brutally steep, unpaved, almost unrideable. It resulted in what one rival to *La Gazzetta* described as 'the national pushing festival'. Torriani abandoned that climb after two years, but sought out new ones and moved the finish to Como, set right among these hills.

Eddy Merckx, who won it twice, described it as "alongside Liège-Bastogne-Liège, the most demanding race on the calendar". Its palmarès has reflected this, featuring the best Classics riders as well as legendary Grand Tour winners, including Felice Gimondi, Roger De Vlaeminck, Bernard Hinault and Sean Kelly. However, in the 1990s and 2000s, 'the race of the falling leaves' lost its lustre, partly as a result of the finish being switched back to Milan and other locations to the south of the hills and partly because of a lack of interest from the sport's biggest names, who weren't interested in racing that hard that late in the season.

The race's fortunes changed in 2004, when the finish returned to Como. In 2012, following the race's rebranding as Il Lombardia, the Muro di Sormano was reinstated, the climb now beautifully surfaced and turned into an art installation that pays tribute to the climb's infamous history and details with agonising precision each individual metre of elevation gained. Switching between finishing in Bergamo and Como, the race has been revitalised.

CHAPTER 3 – THE RACES
IN A NUTSHELL

For men and women the bigger, older one-day road races are known as Classics, and the biggest, oldest and most prestigious of those, called Monument Classics. Another important one-day race is the World Championships. Multi-day stage races have a similar hierarchy, for men at least, led by the three-week Grand Tours, and then smaller events between two and eight days, the more established in Europe and a growing number worldwide.

At Il Lombardia, like so many races, the landscape, towns and villages are amongst the biggest stars of the race

PRO'S PERSPECTIVE

IL LOMBARDIA

*Team BikeExchange-Jayco DS and former
Italian TT champ **Marco Pinotti** on how Il Lombardia
benefited from its 2012 revamp*

"Coming from Bergamo, I'm biased about Lombardia. It's always one of my favourites, one of the most beautiful of the season.

"Races like Il Lombardia are Monuments because they've developed certain patterns over the decades. So, even if you change the start and the finishing town, as long as you maintain key parts of the race or the historical climbs, then it will retain its status. Over the last decade, they've alternated between Bergamo and Como, but they always keep the historic points, particularly the Ghisallo climb. Then, for example last year they did the Passo Ganda coming into Bergamo, whereas in 2016 when Esteban Chaves won, they did the Miragolo San Salvatore, but the heart of the race is always the pre-Alps, medium mountain climbs.

"Also, it's always been 'the race of falling leaves', it's always stayed fixed in that later part of the year. For me, it's as big a race as Liège because of the terrain and because it's the last test of the season. You might not have had a great season, but if you do a great Lombardia you can save it.

"I'd prefer it if they didn't change the course so much, or maybe repeated the route every few years so that fans got more familiar with it. Lombardy is one of the busiest and wealthiest parts of Europe, so I know they design the course with a focus on escaping the traffic. They can't, for instance, start in Milan city centre or use the main roads. They use smaller roads, looking for something different. They do find these climbs that both test the riders and underline that Lombardy, although it's a busy industrial centre, is also a scenic one with all these wonderful places that nobody knows about. One constant, though, is that it's always a course made for great racing, very dynamic."

Marco Pinotti

Six-time Italian Time Trial Champion, Pinotti won stages at the Giro d'Italia and wore the *maglia rosa*. Towards the end of his pro racing career, before moving into coaching, his final appearance at Il Lombardia was marked by a guard of honour at the start in his home town of Bergamo.

Climbing specialist Esteban Chaves took the victory in 2016, beating fellow Colombian Rigoberto Urán and Italy's Diego Rosa

Left *Representing Italy, Marco Pinotti gets encouragement from the fans at the 2013 World Championships Time Trial race in Tuscany,*

Following the explosion in the USA scene, European gravel racing is growing. 2021 saw the first edition of the Serenissima Gravel: 126.8km across northern Italy

GRAVEL 'MONUMENTS'

*Boulder-born **Peter Stetina** shares the low-down on the newest off-road drop-bar races*

It's hard to pick five because in the US there're over 700 gravel races. The golden era of off-road racing is returning, in the US at least, meaning gravel but also ultra-distance mountain biking, which is a part of it, too. The big money series that are starting to emerge are important, they're kind of the headlining shows. But there're also big races like the Mid South and The Steamboat Gravel Race that are independent and proudly so. Then there're the grassroots races, which are the backbone of gravel and were where this all started. So it's about doing it all. But in terms of races where all of the pros show up and could, industry-wise, help get endorsements and all that, here are the big hitters.

1. UNBOUND 100

This is the granddaddy of gravel. It's our Super Bowl, our Tour de France, the unofficial World Championships.

2. STEAMBOAT GRAVEL

In Colorado in August, it's highly prestigious, more like a pro race. There's a big first prize there.

3. THE BELGIAN WAFFLE RIDE

They've franchised it out and have, I believe, four events, with more to come. But California is the highest production value race I've ever done. It's run like the queen stage of the Tour de France. They're making movies around it, there's the tent city, the expo...

4. REBECCA'S PRIVATE IDAHO

A gravel stage race that's run like a mountain bike day – almost – with short, singletracky two-hour events, an uphill time trial, a day off with a party, and then a 100-mile classic gravel grinder.

5. MID SOUTH

This is a passionate race. If the red mud comes, it's a mess. But this year it was cold and like a road race. It's a week of parties, gear releases and bands on stage, and is kind of the season kickoff. If Unbound were Paris-Roubaix, for example, Mid South is a Tour of Flanders – a race for people who are in the know.

Peter Stetina

With his roots deep in road cycling, riding for Garmin-Sharp, BMC and Trek-Segafredo up until 2019, these days, Stetina plies his trade off road at gravel events.

CHAPTER FOUR

TEAMS & RIDERS

How professional cycling leagues are structured and how the teams that race in them are built

❱❱ Professional men's teams fall into three UCI categories. The top teams, for whom the likes of Julian Alaphilippe (Quick-Step Alpha Vinyl Team) and Tadej Pogačar (UAE Team Emirates) race, are known as WorldTeams and compete in the highest designation races on the WorldTour. Teams from lower divisions can also race in WorldTour events when they qualify, usually by earning UCI points, or are granted wildcard entries by race organisers. The second division is known as Professional Continental (including the likes of Mathieu van der Poel at Alpecin-Fenix and Peter Sagan at Team TotalEnergies in 2022). The third division is called Continental.

Unlike other sports such as football, there's no 'pure' promotion and relegation. Instead, the UCI specify that WorldTeam licences, for example, are based on four criteria: ethical, financial, administrative and organisational. Ostensibly, this boils down to ambition and budget. The UCI's rules and regulations lay down myriad requirements for teams in each category. WorldTeams, for instance, must employ "at least 27 riders, four sports directors, coaches, doctors, paramedical assistants, mechanics, etc, on a full-time basis for the whole registration year". They can have up to 30 riders as long as two of them are new professionals.

A maximum of 18 teams are currently allowed to hold WorldTeam status in the men's code, each licence for a three-year period. ProTeams must employ 20 riders, three sports directors and five other staff, while Continental teams must have a minimum of 10 riders (eight for women) and a maximum of 16. The latter can have up to four riders who specialise in other endurance disciplines, such as cyclo-cross, mountain biking and some track events. ❱

⦚ INSTANT EXPERT

CYCLING'S TOP DIVISIONS

Professional men's road cycling comprises three divisions, organised by the sport's world governing body, the UCI:

WORLDTEAMS
(DIVISION 1)

PRO CONTINENTAL
(DIVISION 2)

CONTINENTAL
(DIVISION 3)

After changes introduced by the UCI in 2020 women's pro cycling is a two-tier system.

WORLDTEAMS
(DIVISION 1)

CONTINENTAL
(DIVISION 2)

Roadside fans make cycling a spectacle like no other sport – here the Tour de France riders merge with fans in a giant game of 'Where's Wally' with polka dot jerseys on a Mountains competition summit

Across one-day and stage races, domestiques
duties are varied. Most visible to TV viewers are
the strong riders, shielding their leaders from the
wind, protecting them from other riders, controlling
the pace and watching for attacks to react to

On the women's side, 2022 saw 14 WorldTeams (with riders such as Lotte Kopecky and Marlen Reusser at SD Worx; Elisa Balsamo and Elynor Bäckstedt at Trek-Segafredo) an increase by five from the previous season highlighting the growth of women's road cycling. The regulations also provide full and rather numbing detail on financial, contractual and competitive requirements and restrictions for teams of each type. So let's look instead at how teams are structured in terms of their racing talent and how riders are categorised, albeit in what is a sometimes imprecise manner.

 **JARGON BUSTER**

GRIMPEUR

The specialist climbers who thrive in the mountains, who are typically slim and lightweight, although stronger riders who carry more weight can also succeed with the right power-to weight ratio.

TYPES OF RIDER

Teams are made up from individual riders who have very specific roles, organised to work together

DOMESTIQUE: *THE DUTIFUL SERVANT*

The designation comes from the French word for 'servant', which essentially sums up the role that these riders must fulfil. These dogsbodies of the peloton are charged with doing whatever they can to ensure their leaders reach a race's critical point in the best condition to win it. Those leaders need to be well placed, fresh and as well-fuelled as possible. As a consequence, a team's domestiques will provide a protective shield for them, particularly if they're towards the front or sides of the peloton, in order to shelter them from the wind. They'll be required to drop back to the team car to pick up food and water, or to pick up or return rain jackets and other items of clothing.

In the event of their leader being waylaid by a mechanical incident, the domestiques will stop to pace them back up to the bunch and even hand over a wheel – or even their bike! – at moments when a team car doesn't arrive quickly on the scene. It's not unusual for teams to designate a rider of similar stature to their leader to ride close to their main hitter on a bike that's set up in precisely the same way. After all, while it's fundamental that a leader shouldn't lose ground or time, it rarely matters if a domestique does.

There are different types of domestiques, based on the specific talent they have on the bike. Strong rouleurs will be tasked with acting as their leader's bodyguard, keeping them out of the wind and guiding them through the peloton, as well as with setting the pace on the front of the peloton, either to chase down a breakaway group or to nullify the opportunity for attacks from the bunch. Those that are stronger on climbs will be saved for minding duties and pace-setting on the hills. Those with the ability to sustain a high output of power over significant distances and/or a strong finishing kick in a sprint will be drafted into their sprinter's lead-out 'train', a human-powered locomotive that's intended to increase its speed gradually until it's going full bore at the moment when the sprinter has to make their final acceleration to the line.

"Domestiques do whatever they can to keep their leaders in the best condition to win"

❯

It might sound slightly demeaning and even thankless work, and this may often prove the case, but good domestiques are highly valued in this the most altruistic of team sports. Ever since Jean Dargassies and Henri Gauban were first employed by Henri Pepin to fill this role for him during the 1907 Tour de France, the two domestiques pacing their paymaster from one good restaurant and hotel to the next with almost no regard for the competitive aspect of the race, every one of the peloton's stars has stood on the shoulders of less-heralded, and even completely unheralded, teammates who helped put them in the position to achieve glory.

Two-time Tour de France winner Fausto Coppi had a whole stable of *gregarii*, as they are known in Italy, to ensure *Il Campionissimo* maintained his pre-eminent status over his rivals. Eddy Merckx counted on that same absolute loyalty. In the modern era, the best domestiques are still highly prized and may even be leaders themselves. A good example is Michał Kwiatkowski at Ineos Grenadiers, pacing Chris Froome, Geraint Thomas and Egan Bernal up long climbs at the Tour de France. "He's sacrificing his personal objectives" is often the cry. Yes, but a multi-million euro salary makes that easier to bear.

Luke Rowe is another rider from the British team who's renowned for the spade work he puts in for others.

ROAD CAPTAIN: *READING THE ROAD*

There's sometimes a perception that pro racers are being moved around like chess pieces by sports directors sitting in team cars in the convoy behind the peloton. These managers-cum-puppeteers use TV pictures, real-time data from power meters and other technology, and earpieces that provide them with a link to their riders to carry out their strategies. Yet, although sports directors do work out and explain strategy and tactics before a race, detailing where they want their riders to be at particular times and what to do in these situations, once a race gets under way they're often unable to track what's going on within the peloton, let alone provide instant decisions to their riders. That's a result of TV pictures that are slightly delayed and the near-impossibility of knowing where their riders are positioned within the bunch when unforeseen incidents, usually a crash or an unexpected tactic employed by a rival team, occurs.

In these situations, they rely above all on their team's road captain, an experienced racer who can provide them with 〉

DAN'S VIEW
ON HIMSELF

"My fleeting time in the upper echelons of professional cycling saw me race for Cervélo TestTeam, cum Garmin-Cervélo, between 2009 and 2011. I rode as a domestique, the highlight of which – if you can call three weeks of pain, sleepless nights and exhaustion a 'highlight' – was completing the 2010 Tour de France in support of Carlos Sastre. Carlos won the 2008 Tour de France but finished down in 19th in 2010. How much of that dip in form was down to his support team, well, you'd have to ask Carlos!"

JARGON BUSTER
ROULEUR

These are the strong women and men of the peloton. Without sounding offensive, they're not exceptional at any specific discipline but above normal in each. Their all-round ability aligned with dependability means they often fall into the role of domestique.

Even after a crash, domestiques' duties include fetching food and drinks for their team leaders who must conserve their energy

Team Ineos' success in Grand Tours has relied on strong riders setting the pace to 'control' the race to their leader's advantage

A gifted all-rounder with an amazing climbing ability, Alberto Contador's Grand Tour success owes much to his ability to 'read' a race. Here in the 2015 Giro d'Italia, Mikel Landa won the stage but Contador strengthened his grip on the GC

critical details and, in many cases, take a quick decision when a strategic plan starts to unravel. At ProTeam Alpecin-Fenix, Michael Gogl often takes on this role. "I'd say that you are the voice of the riders in the race. It's a big responsibility," says the Austrian. "The team are aware that I maintain an overview of what's going on during a race, which teams are doing what, where our riders are and how they're feeling, and this puts me in a position to take decisions.

"The sports director doesn't know what's going on, and some riders have a real feel for how a race is unfolding and what might happen next," Gogl continues. "I actually got into this role pretty early. When I was a first-year pro at [the now-disbanded] Tinkoff, I was selected to race alongside our team leader Alberto Contador at the Critérium du Dauphiné and from that moment on I was always the man entrusted with guiding him in races. The team quickly realised that I could be trusted in this position and I've kept it ever since more or less."

"There's constant communication between the lead sports director and riders, particularly the team captain"

It's extremely unusual for a new professional to be given the job of looking after the interests of a multiple Grand Tour winner like Contador but, says Gogl, his ability to 'read' a race has been apparent since his junior racing days. "I've always had a good feel for tactics and how a race will play out, and especially when it comes to foreseeing difficult situations," he explains. "Part of the role involves looking in advance at the roads and other conditions that might have an effect on the race, so that you know when you need to be in a strong position, when to keep your leader in the best position possible, just in case the shit hits the fan, as they say."

Gogl says that there's constant communication between the lead sports director in the convoy just behind the race and the riders, and particularly the team captain, all of them working to a strategy that's been put together the evening before and fully explained in the briefing that takes place on the team bus before the riders line up to race. "We try to work out our tactics in advance and a good part of that comes from attempting to predict what other teams might do. However, there are 22 teams ❯

PRO'S PERSPECTIVE

DIRECTING DECISIONS
Michael Gogl

"During the 2020 Tour de France, we were predicting that the stage [seven] from Millau to Lavaur would end with a bunch finish, where we would work for our sprinter, Giacomo Nizzolo. But Bora [-Hansgrohe] decided to go full gas on the first climb soon after the start, quickly causing a split in the bunch. They kept pulling all day and then when we raced into a crosswind section, it was a mess. There were only about 40 riders in the front group heading towards the finish and we'd lost our initial leader for the stage. So we switched tactics and gave that role to Edvald Boasson Hagen, who ended up taking second place on the stage behind Wout van Aert. That was a good example of us making a quick decision, deciding Edvald would be our protected man that day and it paying off."

in most races, so there are 22 different tactics, which means that sometimes you are right with your predictions, but other times you're not. It's on those occasions when things start to deviate from the script you're expecting that you have to start making decisions within the race. If it's possible, we still communicate with the sports director. But if it isn't, you need to make a decision fast and it's generally up to the road captain to do that," Gogl explains.

It's no coincidence that riders who carve a niche as road captains often end up as sports directors when they retire from racing. This is a move that Gogl can see himself making. "I enjoy having the road captain's role, it's a responsibility and I take it very seriously. Although I'm still quite young and focusing on my career, I do think moving into a new role as a sports director could be an option for me in the future," he says.

LEAD-OUT: *THE SPRINTER'S BEST FRIEND*

Bunch sprints encapsulate perfectly the 'all-for-one' ethos that is so fundamental to success in bike racing. While it's the sprinters, or one of them at least, who ends up savouring success, it often requires a string of teammates to put them in the ideal position for them to achieve this. The riders that form this lead-out 'train' are each allocated a specific role, one or two are given the job of closing down breakaways. One or two more are charged with setting the pace in the closing kilometres. Once the bunch has passed beneath the red kite that marks the start of the final kilometre, another rider tends to lead till 400-500 metres out, when the final lead-out rider, the so-called 'pilot fish', will take the speed up another notch while at the same time looking for the best position for the sprinter to make their final dash.

At the 2022 Eschborn-Frankfurt, Bora-Hansgrohe's Danny van Poppel celebrates every bit as much as the sprinter he led out, Sam Bennett

These riders have often been sprinters themselves, but are not quite quick, daring or agile enough to compete with and, critically, beat the very best. As a consequence, they adapt by taking on the lead-out role, devoting their pure speed and skills for the very best sprinters. Australia's Mark Renshaw fulfilled this role for Mark Cavendish for many years. More recently, Denmark's Michael Mørkøv has proved devastatingly effective as the final locomotive in Deceuninck-QuickStep's lead-out train, combining successfully with Fernando Gaviria, Elia Viviani, Sam Bennett, and with Mark Cavendish to devastating effect at the 2021 Tour de France, where the Manxman won four stages and the green jersey.

> *"Bunch sprints encapsulate perfectly the 'all-for-one' ethos that's fundamental to success"*

SPRINTER DELIVERY

The understanding between lead-out and sprinter is vital. Sometimes the relationship can click quickly and others develop over time – it's not uncommon for pairs or trios to switch teams as a group to maintain their partnership. Here sprinter Mark Cavendish is unleashed by his regular lead-out man, Mark Renshaw while they were at Etixx-QuickStep.

MANON'S VIEW

TEAM INSTRUCTIONS

"In every race you do as a pro you will be given a job. Your job won't always be to win, it might be to look after the race's leader in the first half of the race and make sure she is safe and protected; it might be to get in the break; or it might be to be the last rider in the lead-out train. No matter what your job is in the race, once you have successfully done it you feel like it's a win!"

Miguel Indurain is rightly celebrated for his five Tour de France wins in the 1990s, but his TT power also earned him World and Olympic titles, and the World Hour Record

'Super' Mario Cipollini may be remembered as fondly for his outlandish skinsuits as for his 170 pro victories, including 42 Giro stages

STAT ATTACK!
TT KINGS & QUEENS

Going into the 2022 season these riders had the most WorldTour-level time trial wins

MEN
Since the ProTour was established in 2005:

26: Fabian **Cancellara**

24: Tony **Martin**

15: Rohan **Dennis**

WOMEN
Since the Women's WorldTour was established in 2016:

13: Annemiek **van Vleuten**

3: Ellen **van Dijk** and Lisa **Brennauer**

No other riders have won more than one WWT level time trial during this period, such is Van Vleuten's dominance.

LEGENDS OF THE SPORT
MARIO CIPOLLINI

Italian **Mario Cipollini** was the archetypal sprinter, his brashness matched by his success, 'Il Re Leone' (The Lion King) winning 170 times. 'Cipo' wasn't shy either, his skinsuits including leopard print and 'skeleton' (left).

SPRINTER: *THE FASTEST WHEELS*

Like strikers on a football team, sprinters are judged by the number of times they throw their arms up to celebrate success. The best of them might claim as many as two dozen victories over the course of a season, but just a handful taken on the most important races can be enough to enable a sprinter to maintain their elite status.

Shepherded from the very start of a race to within 200 metres or so of the finish line, sprinters are more conscious than any other type of rider of the need to maintain every watt of power until those decisive final metres. (See more on p134.)

TIME-TRIALLIST: *STRONG AND STREAMLINED*

Just as some riders are born to climb mountains quickly, others are predisposed to powering big gears over extended distances, ranging from the handful of kilometres that are typical of prologue time trials to courses of up to 50km and more that comprise the longer time trials that are programmed on Grand Tours. Specialist time-triallists, such as Italian phenomenon Filippo Ganna, tend to be among the bigger riders in the peloton, their innate strength providing them with the ability to push bigger gears than smaller riders, making them faster.

However, while basic power is crucial to time-trial success, other factors also play a key part when racing on your own against the clock, particularly bike set-up and the rider's position. The first of these factors derives to a large extent from the second. Being aerodynamic is important, but it can be a handicap if the position that's adopted doesn't allow the rider to produce optimum power output. As a consequence, a compromise has to be reached and it's one that riders who have been blooded on the track are among the best at making, Ganna being one of them, but also Tour de France winners Bradley Wiggins and Geraint Thomas, who were both world and Olympic track champions before switching their focus to the road.

Yet this needn't always be the case. Some riders simply find that they're perfectly suited to riding as hard as possible for as long as possible, Alex Dowsett among them. The British time-trial scene has always been very vibrant, often eclipsing road racing, and it was by riding the 10- and 25-mile time trials that are the staple of this scene that Dowsett's talent was nurtured and, eventually, led to him winning a time-trial at the Giro d'Italia, finishing on the podium at the World Time Trial Championship and, in 2015, breaking the World Hour Record. (See more on p136.) ❯

A cluster of climbers: Deceuninck-QuickStep's João Almeida and Jumbo-Visma's George Bennett eye Simon Yates of Team BikeExchange as he gets out of the saddle to pile on the pressure in the 2021 Giro d'Italia

CLIMBER: *LIGHTWEIGHT POWERHOUSE*

Before revealing what makes a world-class climber, it's worth noting that every professional rider *can* climb. A sprinter like Mark Cavendish or Sam Bennett, for instance, may be labelled as a non-climber, but that's a relative term based on their specialist ability and the ability of the climbing specialists they keep company with... they're still able to complete the toughest of Grand Tour climbing stages often within 40 minutes or so of the best climbers in the sport.

Traditionally, the riders categorised as climbers tended to be small or at least very slight and to have little chance of contesting the main prize in Grand Tours and other major stage races. Unable to defend their chances in time-trials and, often, even follow the pace on flat stages, they came into their own when the mountains loomed, usually becoming involved in a contest

LEGENDS OF THE SPORT
GINO BARTALI

Seven-times a Giro d'Italia Mountains Classification winner, Bartali won the Giro GC three times and the Tour de France GC twice in the 1930s and 40s. Bartali used training rides as a cover for secret efforts to help Jewish people during WW2 and was posthumously honoured.

'The Badger', five-times Tour de France winner Bernard Hinault, on his way to becoming World Champion in 1980

between themselves rather than having an influence or impact on the general classification.

At the same time, though, and since the early days of the sport, stage-race specialists have needed to be strong on the climbs even if they are not the lightest. Going back to the 1930s and 1940s, legendary Italian riders Gino Bartali and Fausto Coppi forged their many Grand Tour triumphs in the mountains, Bartali relying on his devastating acceleration and brute strength, Coppi depending more on his pedalling technique and ability to keep a big gear turning even when going uphill.

> ## *"Power climbers like to set a high pace and stick to it, avoiding changes in rhythm"*

Essentially, this pair are the models for the two different types of climber. Following in Coppi's wheeltracks have been the likes of Jacques Anquetil, Eddy Merckx, Bernard Hinault and, more recently, Bradley Wiggins and Geraint Thomas, riders described by the French as *rouleurs-grimpeurs*, essentially power climbers who like to set a high pace and stick to it, avoiding too many changes in rhythm.

Bartali's successors, meanwhile, are the *grimpeurs purs*, specialist climbers who not only cope with frequent changes of tempo, but rely on short bursts of speed to drop and defeat their rivals, and epitomised by riders such as Federico Bahamontes, José ❯

Manuel Fuente, Lucien Van Impe and, in more contemporary times, Alberto Contador and Nairo Quintana.

Warren Barguil is another who fits the Bartali template. Winner of the two mountain stages and the red polka-dot King of the Mountains jersey at the 2017 Tour de France, the slender Frenchman has come to know his limits. Barguil chased dreams of Grand Tour glory, but was ultimately let down by his inability in time-trials. He's now turned his focus back to climbing, realising, like so many have before him, that fans will always offer acclaim to racers who can provide unpredictability. (See more on p138.)

STAGE-RACE LEADER: *ALL-ROUND EXCELLENCE*

The peloton's elite, stage-race leaders need all kinds of qualities to succeed. With regard to racing ability, they have to be able to climb well, while most of them are good time-triallists as well. Riders blessed with those skills also have to know when to make best use of them and, as a result, when they need to be patient. In a contest that ultimately boils down to being the most durable and committing your energy resources when there's likely to be the best return, stage racers spend most of their time following others – their teammates, principally, who lead them around the bunch,

"For the best stage racers, success is often about forgetting flamboyance, and keeping control"

keeping them out of the wind as much as possible, fetching food, water and clothing, but also tracking their rivals at key points, most obviously on the climbs, but also when the wind threatens to disrupt or the road conditions could produce some kind of unforeseen event.

For the best stage racers, success is often about forgetting flamboyance and racing on feel, and being conservative and keeping control, usually via your teammates. A common gripe about stage-race leaders is that they often don't show any panache. Yet, if they were to, their chances of stage-race success would almost certainly diminish. The key thing they have to learn is self-control, to rein themselves in, as this is fundamental to their hopes of success. Doing this, however, won't gain them universal acclaim from fans. (See more on p140.)

Marianne Vos' drive for success in both one-day and stage races is insatiable. There is no hiding her delight at sprinting to victory on this stage of the 2021 Simac Ladies Tour

LEGEND IN THE MAKING

Mathieu van der Poel *launched himself into cycling folklore on a grey spring day in Belgium...*

Some call it the greatest ambush in cycling. Others simply the greatest Classic moment of the modern area. It was early 2019 and, after shining in cyclo-cross and mountain biking, cycling fans awaited Mathieu van der Poel's efforts at transferring his off-road talents to the road. The Dutch rider had already served notice of his road potential by winning competitive races Dwars door Vlaanderen and Brabantse Pijl. But the Amstel Gold Race, a Classic in late April, was a step up again. Could Van der Poel make the grade?

It seemed not as, with 10km to go, he was out of the picture and over a minute down on leaders Julian Alaphilippe and Jakob Fuglsang. With 3km to go, the lead had shrunk to 35 seconds. Better but still insurmountable. Still, a podium place at one of the world's greatest races wasn't a bad day's work...

Or better still, victory. Incredibly, Van der Poel, seemingly projected from a powerful catapult, launched a memorable sprint with 200m to go that Alaphilippe and Fuglsang simply couldn't live with. Van der Poel, as he's done throughout his cycling career, had done it — he'd made the impossible possible.

The grandson of Raymond Poulidor – eight times a Tour de France podium finisher – Mathieu van der Poel impresses in every discipline he races

THE CLASSICS CHAMPION

Just as almost every Classic is different, there's no one type of Classics rider. Broadly, there are two groups, those who prefer the cobbled Classics and those that lean towards the hilly Classics, although, just like the races, some riders will bridge this divide.

Mads Pedersen is a good example of a rider who's perfectly cut out for the cobbled Classics, such as the Ronde van Vlaanderen, Paris-Roubaix and Gent-Wevelgem. Tall and strong, the Dane can power short climbs as quickly as almost anyone, has the body weight to keep him stable on the cobbles and, often crucially for him, relishes racing when the conditions are at their worst. Winner of the 2019 World Road Race Championship in the monsoon conditions that hit Yorkshire, Pedersen is also blessed with a prodigious finishing kick and, vitally, a canny instinct for tactics.

While some exceptional riders such as Wout van Aert, Julian Alaphilippe and Mathieu van der Poel do bridge the divide and can contend in the hilly Classics as well, most of their rivals in these events won't be seen towards the front end of a one-day race until the Ardennes Classics of Amstel Gold, Flèche Wallonne and Liège-Bastogne-Liège in mid-April. The courses of these races and Il Lombardia are comparable to the hardest Grand Tour stages. There's lots of climbing and success tends to depend on judging the right time to move. Unlike De Ronde and, particularly, Roubaix, it's now almost unheard of for a rider to win one of the hilly Classics with a long-range break. (See more on p142.)

CHAPTER 4 – TEAMS & RIDERS
IN A NUTSHELL

Road racing is a team sport where individuals earn most of the success and take most of the plaudits – but the support of domestiques and lead-out riders, the expertise of a road captain, and the work done by backroom staff, all play a hugely significant role in enabling that one rider to cross the line first. Cyclo-cross and gravel racing are quite different, however. Although team strategy can come into play, the racers are essentially on their own, in a similar way to the pioneering road racers in the late 19th and early 20th centuries. It's each racer – and their bike – against the rest. Thus these disciplines are perhaps purer, but lack the tactical complexity and to a large extent the unpredictability of road racing.

"There are those who prefer the cobbled Classics and those that lean towards the hilly Classics"

PRO'S PERSPECTIVE

THE SPRINTER

*QuickStep-Alpha Vinyl's **Mark Cavendish** is the very model of a top-level sprinter*

"My sensations in sprints have changed as I've got older. When I was younger, I didn't feel any fear. In fact, I didn't really feel any emotion. I thought of emotion as kind of a waste of energy... Any emotion, of joy or anger say, was taken away from the process of sprinting. Instead of seeing other riders there I just saw the gaps.

"I honestly didn't feel pressure to win. I was a World Champion when I was 19 [The Madison, 2005 Olympics, with Rob Hayles] and after that I was expected to win as an amateur, and then I turned pro and was winning straight away, and was expected to win... Quite quickly, I thought that was normal, I thought that was what everyone felt because I didn't know any different.

"For me, bunch sprinting is the only part of the sport left that uses pure tactics. Even a mountain stage is literally a time trial where everyone starts together. It's a physical thing. You can deal with it or you can't, it's as simple as that. You know what power you can put out and you can do that, and whoever can hold the highest threshold wins. Sprinting is a lot more dynamic than that. Maybe not much happens in the stage early on, but that's because they know it's going to be a bunch sprint [at the finish].

"Tour de France sprints are always different. The majority of the peloton are there for GC goals and there's a lot less guys up there in the sprints. There's a lot more up there till 3km to go, but in the last 3km there are a fair few less than in other races. In most other races, teams will go with a full sprint team, but at the Tour they don't. But the other difference is that everyone who is there is in peak form, so the sprints are faster, there's more going on. I always approach the Tour de France differently. The Tour de France is my life, I owe my career to the Tour de France. I've won a lot of races. But even if I'd won everything, if I hadn't won at the Tour it wouldn't have counted for shit, to be fair."

Mark Cavendish

'The Manx Missile' is one of cycling's all-time great sprinters, with Points Classification wins at all three Grand Tours and a record-equalling 34 stage wins at the Tour de France after 2021's comeback. Cav's honours include a road World Championships, multiple track World Championships and an Olympic silver in the Omnium at Rio, behind Elia Viviani.

Above 'Cav' cemented his status with a dramatic comeback at the 2021 Tour de France, including victory in the 13th stage into Carcassonne

Mark Cavendish cut his teeth on the track, and continued to race in GB colours, here, winning the Madison at the 2016 World Championships with Bradley Wiggins

PRO'S PERSPECTIVE

THE TIME TRIALLIST

*Israel-Premier Tech's **Alex Dowsett** on
what it takes to be a champion time triallist*

"I think you've got to love it. I think you've got to enjoy the
process of trying to go fast for a long time, but also the sensation
of being at your limit and staying there. I think you have to enjoy
– I wouldn't say it's suffering, although there is an element of
suffering to it, but I don't think it's about that. It's trying to solve
this scientific experiment to try to maximise speed, to cover a
certain distance at the fastest possible speed. It's not like road
racing where you're trying to outwit your opponents in the
moment. In time trialling, you're just trying to be the better, the
faster cyclist. It's about self-improvement rather than trying to
mess up someone else in the hope of beating them.

"I've always preferred time trialling to road racing. It was how
I started. I think I enjoyed it because I was good at it. It was
something that I went back to every week and tried to be better
than I was the week before. It was quite methodical because it
was often the same course, the same stretch of road, and often
it'd be similar conditions. So you're trying to better yourself in a
similar way to running, certainly like track and field running. It was
the closest to that, because you often have the same conditions,
and it was quite a short effort as well. When you compare it to
road racing, I like the purity of time trialling. Nine times out of
10, unless the conditions change dramatically after the start, the
fastest person won, and I liked that idea. It took a while for me to
get my head round road racing, about the fact that you could not
be the best person in the race and win, or you could be the best
cyclist in the race and not win seemed a little pointless to me.

"Doing lead-outs has benefited my time trialling and vice versa.
I just have to make sure that I've got the punchier aspects of the
lead-out dialled because you have to go over your limit. So they
certainly go hand in hand. A lead-out is a sustained effort at the
end of the race and under a certain amount of fatigue as well."

Alex Dowsett

Six-time British national TT
champion rider Alex Dowsett
includes a Giro d'Italia ITT
stage win on his palmarès as
well as breaking the World
Hour Record in 2015 at the
Manchester Velodrome.

The skill and confidence to maintain high speed while cornering is key to TT success – it also makes spectacular viewing for fans

Dowsett's metronomic pacing skills came into play when he took an emotional 18km solo breakaway stage victory at the 2020 Giro

After playing an important part in the Jumbo-Visma team (here supporting Steven Kruijswijk on the Tourmalet at the 2019 Tour de France), Bennett is now crucial in Tadej Pogačar's Team UAE Emirates success

INSTANT EXPERT

THE COL DU TOURMALET

The Col du Tourmalet is a famous Tour de France climb in the Pyrenees. By 2020 it had featured a total of 87 times since 1910 when the first rider to conquer it was Octave Lapize, who went on to win that edition's General Classification. On the climb there is a statue of the Frenchman, who died being shot down as a fighter pilot in WW1.

The Tourmalet has also featured in the Vuelta a España several times.

On days where he's granted race leader status, Bennett likes to unleash, like in the Autumn Classic, Gran Piemonte, winning in 2020

PRO'S PERSPECTIVE

THE CLIMBER

*UAE Team Emirates' **George Bennett** on what makes a top-level climber different to other riders...*

"Mentally, you need to be able to really hurt yourself for a long time, and that's also a drawback of being a climber. You're often on the limit, you're skinny and you get sick and all that stuff. Physically you need, obviously, to be light and powerful, but you do lose in other aspects of racing. For instance, unless you're Tadej Pogačar or Primož Roglič, when you're good at the 40-minute climbs, you do lose speed in other areas. Because of the way I train, I don't have much of a finishing kick, so to win races, I have to drop everybody. One of the other difficult things that you have to get used to is that you have to spend a lot of time training at altitude, you spend a lot of time training on these climbs, and that's not easy from a psychological standpoint. I don't think there's an easy sort of vocation in cycling, but at the same time I think climbing is definitely one of the harder ones.

"When it comes to racing, we're not like sprinters who, if they miss out one day, can go with all they've got at the next opportunity and keep doing that in a Grand Tour. If a climber misses their opportunity on a mountain stage, they've lost completely. You've got to pick and choose your opportunities really carefully. If you're riding for GC as well, you've got to be alert on the flat days, you've got to be good at everything."

Bennett has raced all three Grand Tours multiple times, and shares his love for the Tour de France... but why?
"It's the Tour de France! For a start, it's why I ride a bike. I think it's the race that got me into cycling. When I was a mountain biker, I didn't know any other road race than the Tour de France and that's stuck with me. That's what I dream about, it's what I build my season around... The Tour has the big mountains as well, and I just love the Alps and the Pyrenees. I love the Tour and being a climber in the Tour. I mean, shit doesn't get better than that does it?"

George Bennett

A seasoned campaigner and national road champion, Bennett became the first New Zealander to win a WorldTour event, the 2017 Tour of California, where his performance on climbing stages made the difference, and which he secured with the final individual time trial.

Chris Froome's 2017 Tour de France victory was his third successive and fourth overall

With his 80km solo to win stage 19 in 2018, Froome became the first Briton to win the Giro d'Italia

PRO'S PERSPECTIVE

THE STAGE RACER

*In stage racing, there are few more successful
than Israel-Premier Tech's **Chris Froome***

"It was only towards the end of 2011 that I really started to
understand how to ride my bike properly in the bunch, whereas
now when I'm racing I think about every little piece of energy, and
every pedal stroke that's under my threshold, saving energy, if
you like. Throughout the day I'm thinking constantly, 'I want to try
and pedal as easily as possible until I have to really go,' And then
I put everything into it," Froome told *Wired*.

"In training I'd go out and do these great efforts. I could see the
power was very high, higher than a lot of my teammates on the
climbs, but then I'd get to the race, and because of the way I ride
I wouldn't be sat in a very good position. I'd be moving around the
bunch a lot, I'd be sometimes attacking at the beginning of the
stage, things like that, just wasting energy.

"When it really came to the climbs, where it counts, where the
race was won or lost, I just wouldn't have it. It was like, 'He can
do it in training, but when it comes to the races he's not there,
he's getting dropped.' So I knew that just didn't add up. I think that
learning to ride in the bunch is a huge thing that's underestimated.
You think, 'He can hold a certain power, put him in a bike race and
he'll win.' But cycling is so much more dynamic, it's about fighting
for position, it's about holding good positions, not wasting energy
through the stage. I had to learn all of these little things."

In *Full Gas*, Peter Cossins' award-winning book on tactics,
Froome further explained his approach: "Tactics are something
that I've thought a lot about and especially after realising that,
great as it is sometimes to be the strongest guy and just use
the simple tactic of waiting until the hardest moment and then
pushing on, there are moments when you maybe don't feel like
the strongest guy and those are the times when you really have
to rely on tactics over pure brute force to win you the race."

Chris Froome

One of only seven riders (and
the most recent) to have won
GC on all three Grand Tours,
Froome won the Critérium du
Dauphiné in 2013, 2015 and
2016 in preparation for three
of his four Tour de France
victories. It was on a training
ride during the 2019 Dauphiné
that the Brit suffered life-
threatening injuries, since
when he hasn't hit the same
heights of performance.

PRO'S PERSPECTIVE

THE CLASSICS SPECIALIST

*Israel-Premier Tech's **Michael Woods** compares his love for Classics with the pressure of GC*

"I love the Ardennes Classics because they're just so hard. They're so challenging, mentally and physically. They're unrelenting. And to be a winner there, you have to be a really complete bike rider, especially now with the new Liège course the way it is, so that it no longer finishes on an uphill but down in the city. You have to be not only strong, but also tactically adept. Even at Flèche Wallonne, although it's a climbers' finish, you have to be in a really good position to win it. You just have to be a complete rider to win, and that's why I like them. I love Amstel, too, for the same reasons. It's not been the best place for me, but it's such a sweet race.

Woods also acknowledges the different pressures that come with stage races, be that riding for GC or focusing on stage wins. "Ever since I came into the sport, I've always hunted for stage wins, that's kind of always been the theme. In chasing that goal, I've also done some good GC rides in the past. Ultimately, though, when you have guys like Pogačar and Roglič who have very few chinks in their armour it's very difficult to compete, especially as I do have a chink in my armour, which is the time trial. Although I've improved on that, it's still difficult for me to win a Grand Tour, whereas winning stages is something that's really important to me. I care less about coming in the top 10 than getting a stage victory, so that's why my goals lie there.

"I've done GC and I've done stage hunting, and both have their different pressures. GC is more of a slow burn and if you play it smart, although it's a lot of pressure, it's also a nice challenge at the same time. It's less intense, you just have to be more cerebral. Whereas when you're chasing stages, although you have a lot of time to switch off, when you have to be on, there's a tonne of pressure. You have less room for error, you have to execute on the day, and that comes with a number of pressures as well."

Michael Woods

Having won both Milano-Torino and stages at the Vuelta a España during his time at EF Education, Canadian Woods has also podium'd at Liège-Bastogne-Liège, La Flèche Wallonne and the 2018 World Championships, which featured 5000m of climbing over the 265km course at Innsbruck, Austria.

Above Woods and Alejandro Valverde both won stages at the 2022 Gran Camiño, with the Spaniard overhauling the Canadian's slender GC lead on the final day

Woods won the 100th edition of Milano-Torino in 2019, pipping Alejandro Valverde

PRO'S PERSPECTIVE

THE CYCLO-CROSS RACER

*Baloise-Trek Lions' **Lucinda Brand** on what makes a cyclo-cross rider*

"I started to do cyclo-cross because my dad said that I had to train in the winter to have good form for the first races in the road season. So, little me jumped into the local club races in the mud on a Sunday and as I began to do more of them I really started to like it. That led to me doing some other local races, and then to a national championship. Then when I became a leading rider on the road, people started to tell me that it was hard to combine the two disciplines. So I basically just did a few races in December as training, for fun really. Then, I think in the last year that Rabobank sponsored my team in 2016, I decided to do a proper 'cross season... So that was basically the start of what's now become a situation where I share my racing time between two teams.

"First of all, you need to be – or need to learn to be – a good bike handler. That comes naturally over time, because if you feel like you have control over your bike, it does become less scary. Secondly, you need a lot of power. You need to be able to produce strong interval efforts, to be quick, explosive, able to push hard, then have a really short recovery and be able to go again. I think those are the two most important things.

"You can save so much time and energy by running because it's a key part of the sport. For the most part, the sections you have to run aren't that long. The key thing when you're remounting is to carry some speed while jumping on, and clipping into your pedals quickly, to maintain your momentum. In the past, I did have to close lots of gaps after sections where you had to run. Thankfully, though, I've become better at it."

Lucinda Brand
A world, European and multiple national Netherlands champion for Elite Women's Cyclo-cross, Brand rides in the CX season for the Baloise-Trek-Lions team – managed by Sven Nys, winner of 50 CX World Cup races – and in the road season for Trek-Segafredo.

Bike handling and technical skills such as dismounting and running make CX a challenging discipline and great fun for fans to watch

PRO'S PERSPECTIVE

ESPORTS CHAMPION

Ashleigh Moolman Pasio on levelling the playing field

"One big advantage of eSports is the potential to grow female participation. It's so much less intimidating for women to start in the safety of their own home and to test their boundaries, because one of the limitations for women in cycling is that it's intimidating to get started. There are so many things to worry about. Am I going to embarrass myself? What if I crash? What if I puncture? Am I going to be dropped? eSports allows them to try things out in a safe environment and grow their confidence, and then hopefully take the next step to competing in the real world."

Team SD Worx were the UCI number 1 ranked Women's WorldTour team in 2021

CHAPTER FIVE

THE BUSINESS END

Running a professional cycling team is unlike any other sport. Here's how the money works

>> Cycling has an unusual business model that is beset by a fundamental flaw: income can't be generated through spectator ticket sales so teams are dependent on sponsors. While some of these deals are long term – such as Sky funding its team for almost a decade – most cover no more than four seasons, creating an inherent lack of stability that, according to many, makes it unfit for purpose.

The teams court prospective sponsors, highlighting the visibility their brand will achieve; the cost and length of the sponsorship deal is agreed; towards the end of the term, the two parties either extend the deal or part ways. If it's the latter, the courting process begins again, hopefully for a new, improved deal. Yet – and here's where the flaw manifests itself, creating uncertainty for teams, riders and staff – there may be less money or even none at all.

There's long been talk of overhauling this system, by giving teams a cut of TV rights money, for instance, but race organisers have been adamant that they won't countenance this. In 2014, ten WorldTour teams formed Velon, a group seeking to reform the financial model and boost income from other sources, including selling on-bike footage and broadcast rights to its own races, the Hammer Series.

Steeped in the historic imbalance in their development the financing of the top levels of men's and women's cycling are currently at very different levels. But that is changing. ❯

HOW MUCH RIDERS EARN

Riders' income is made up from salaries, personal endorsement deals and prize money

» **From the team:** Riders' salaries demonstrate the differences between top-level men's and women's riders, and also reflects how the women's sport is currently updating.

In 2021, elite level men's WorldTeams had to pay their riders a minimum annual wage of €40,045 (for contracted employees) or €65,673 (for self-employed contractors). The minimum wage at men's ProTeam level was €32,100, with no minimum requirement at Continental level. In the same season, Women's WorldTeams' minimum salary was €20,000 (employed) or €32,800 (self-employed), rising to €27,500/€45,100 in 2022 and to equal the ProTeam minimum in 2023. In addition to health and life insurance, maternity benefits and paid holiday, teams in this category were also required to contribute to a pension plan from 2022. These reforms were intended to bring minimum pay in line with the men's ProTeam level by 2023, although some teams, including Trek-Segafredo and Team BikeExchange, took this step in 2021. In women's Continental teams, around 25% of racers were unpaid.

At the top end of the wage scale, salaries for the biggest names in men's cycling compare with stars in other sports. The highest paid rider in 2021 was UAE Team Emirates leader Tadej Pogačar, reported to have received €6 million, with Chris Froome on €5.5m, Peter Sagan €5m and Geraint Thomas €3.5m. Sprinter Pascal Ackermann reportedly signed for a salary of €1.5m when he joined UAE in 2022, while Spanish climber Marc Soler was said to have boosted his wage to €1.2m when he joined the same team. At the top end the discrepancy between the women's sport and the men's is even more stark than in comparing the minimum salaries. Within the women's peloton, one of the most successful and highest profile riders, Annemiek van Vleuten doubled her salary to €250,000 when she joined Movistar from BikeExchange at the end of 2020 – still a fraction of her male counterparts.

FROM INDIVIDUAL DEALS

These include appearance fees paid by race organisers to a rider or payments made by companies for endorsement of their products. The one occasion where some male riders do earn **›**

Annemiek van Vleuten's performances are returning on Movistar Team's investment in her

TEAM BUDGETS

HOW TEAMS ARE FINANCED

The majority of funding comes from partners including main sponsors who get to 'own' the team name

Along with the title sponsors, bike, clothing, component and nutrition suppliers pay a fee (and supply goods 'in kind') to be visible at the big, globally televised races. This table shows the sizes of teams and their budgets in recent years. While the number of men's teams has dropped the women's has grown significantly, and while men's WorldTour team budgets have grown steadily, women's have doubled, albeit from a low base

WORLDTOUR TEAMS	2020	2021	2022
Number of teams	19	19	18
Total budget (Million Euros)	374	379	430
Average team budget (Million Euros)	19.7	20	23.9
Total number of riders	539	553	511
Total number of staff	909	969	976
Average rider salary (Thousand Euros)	373.6	372.6	402.9

PROTOUR TEAMS	2020	2021	2022
Number of teams	19	19	17
Total budget (Million Euros)	84	87	91.9
Average team budget (Million Euros)	4.4	4.6	5.8
Total number of riders	409	416	377
Total number of staff	320	336	347
Average rider salary (Thousand Euros)	71.3	76.5	80.4

WOMEN'S WORLDTOUR	2020	2021	2022
Number of teams	8	9	14
Total budget (Million Euros)	10.6	14.6	33.2
Average team budget (Million Euros)	1.3	1.6	2.4
Total number of riders	106	117	181
Total number of staff	63	101	123
Average rider salary (Thousand Euros)	41.6	53	61

Sagan's performances over the years and his camera-friendly charm, mean he remains a well rewarded rider

significant amounts for appearing in an event is during the post-Tour de France criterium season. Several decades ago, riders might appear at two of these events a day over the best part of a month. Nowadays, although salaries are much higher and there are fewer of these races, riders still appear in them, with the Tour victor and jersey winners believed to earn around €30,000 per outing. Payments for appearances in UCI-endorsed races are much rarer, but do take place. In 2018, for instance, Chris Froome was reportedly paid €1.4m to appear in the Giro d'Italia.

The details of endorsement deals are kept between a rider and their personal sponsor, but these can be very substantial. US bike manufacturer Specialized committed to paying a significant chunk of Peter Sagan's salary when he joined the Total Energies team on an initial two-year deal in 2022. During the 2020 Tour, meanwhile, Julian Alaphilippe raced wearing a €155,000 Richard Mille watch.

FROM PRIZE MONEY

Compared to tennis or golf, prize money in cycling is small. For example, the total purse for the 2021 men's Ronde van Vlaanderen was €50,000, Kasper Asgreen picking up €20,000 for first place and payments down to the 10th-placed rider (€500). Yet these figures were substantially higher than the prize money on offer for the women's race in 2021, for which the total purse was a mere €7,005, winner Annemiek van Vleuten collecting €1,535. However, from 2022 De Ronde offered equal prize funds of €50,000 to the men's and women's races, with Mathieu van der Poel and Lotte Kopecky each collecting €20,000 for their wins. Race organisers Flanders Classics are offering equal prize money for men's and women's editions of all its races from 2023.

Victory at the 2021 Vuelta a España netted Primož Roglič €150,000. Bahrain-Victorious earned €12,500 for the team prize, Michael Storer received €13,000 as the best climber, while Gino Mäder and Fabian Jakobsen got €11,000 each for the best young rider and points titles, respectively, as did each stage winner.

As it does in so many other ways, the Tour de France stands out as the obvious exception with regard to prize money. In 2021, the purse totalled €2,228,450, yellow jersey winner Tadej Pogačar receiving €500,000 of this. Every rider ranked between Bauke Mollema in 20th place and Tim Declercq, who was 141st and last, received €1,000. Like the Vuelta, a stage win paid out €11,000, while points winner Mark Cavendish and King of the Mountains ❯

Multiple Tour de France winner Chris Froome was reportedly paid €1.4 million to appear in the Giro d'Italia

HOW MUCH TEAM BUDGETS VARY

Looking in more detail at individual teams' budgets, there is a significant discrepancy in scope

WorldTeam budgets in 2021 ranged from the €50 million for Ineos Grenadiers down to Qhubeka-Assos's €8 million pot. The average budget at the top level was around €20 million, with just Ineos, UAE (€35m), Jumbo-Visma (€27m), Deceuninck-QuickStep (€23m), Movistar and Groupama-FDJ (both €20m), matching or topping this mark.

By contrast, in Women's WorldTour racing, budgets ranged from €1m-€3m euros per season. These smaller operations are growing rapidly on average, with the diversity in size of team's budgets looking set to follow the pattern of the men's sport. In both, teams with the bigger budgets attract more of the best riders, and can play out a wider range of strategies if they have more individual riders who have the potential to win.

Budgets at ProTeam level range from the €10 million for Arkéa-Samsic, Total-Direct Energie and Alpecin-Fenix teams in 2021 down to €2 million-€3 million that enabled the Spanish Kern Pharma outfit to step up into this category in 2022.

Women's Continental (the second tier) team budgets range from €100,000 up to the €1 million invested by Cofidis when it established its women's team in 2022.

At men's Continental level (third tier), some teams that focus on a domestic calendar operate on budgets less than €100,000. Others with a more international outlook may have a budget at least five times bigger than this, or more.

Prize money pots vary, with the Tour de France GC winner in 2021 Tadej Pogačar earning €500,000 to be shared with his team

Prize money doesn't always reflect effort: 2021 Tour de France 'lanterne rouge' and relentlessly hard working domestique Tim Declercq bagged €1k

Pogačar each earned €25,000. In contrast, 2022's inaugural Tour de France Femmes had a €250,000 prize fund, substantially bigger than any other race on the calendar but well below the men's purse. The GC winner would earn €50,000 from that total; around one tenth of that for the men.

Cycling also stands apart because the prizes won by individuals are, by tradition, shared between riders and backroom staff. Racers are comfortable with this system because they recognise that every individual's success depends on the support of their teammates, while they can also make some large gains in fees from bonuses, appearances and personal sponsorship deals.

FROM DEAL MAKING?

In a sport where making temporary alliances is a part of the strategic game plan, buying and selling races has a long history... anecdotal accounts suggest some riders earned more by selling races than by winning them. But is this underhand tactic still prevalent? The lack of evidence suggests not. This is not to say that riders don't ask for or give favours in races. There are some sound strategic reasons for collaboration; riders in a break might work together to distance a mutual rival, or a GC-focused rider may concede the stage win to another racer, knowing they'll take the overall lead. At the top level at least, there appears to be little to gain and much to lose from buying or selling a race. ❯

STAT ATTACK!
RACE FINES

Fines are handed out to riders and other team staff for various infringements. In the 2020 Grand Tours these varied from illegal feeding, littering, 'Sticky bottle' (200 Swiss francs for riders; 1,000 for DSs), to 'Inappropriate behaviour in front of public' (typically that's urinating within view of spectators), 'Failing to respect commissionaire instructions', 'Incorrect use of rainbow flag' and 'Assault, threat, insult against UCI member' (2,000 Swiss francs).

REVENUE STRUCTURE
- Sponsors in cash
- Sponsors in kind
- Other revenues

COSTS STRUCTURE
- Personnel
- Vehicles
- Competitions
- General costs
- Other expenses

PERSONNEL EXPENSES
- Staff
- Riders

WORLDTOUR TEAMS

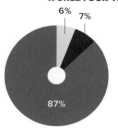

6% 7%
87%

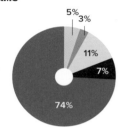

5% 3%
11%
7%
74%

24%
76%

PROTOUR TEAMS

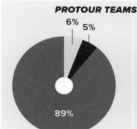

6% 5%
89%

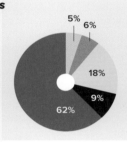

5% 6%
18%
9%
62%

32%
68%

WOMEN'S WORLDTOUR TEAMS

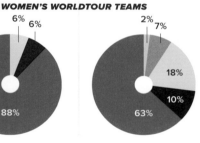

6% 6%
88%

2% 7%
18%
10%
63%

32%
68%

TEAM COSTS

WHERE THE MONEY GOES

A breakdown of where the different types of teams' average costs and expenses are incurred

While the scope of budgets varies across WorldTour, ProTour and Women's WorldTour teams, the way they're funded is largely similar. The costs structure is almost identical between ProTour and Women's WorldTour teams – the biggest difference for WorldTour teams being personnel costs, with more riders, and the highest-paid riders' salaries skewing the averages.

CX & GRAVEL: DIFFERENT MODELS

Spectators' gate receipts and competitors' entry fees mean different models for different disciplines

>> The financial set-up of cyclo-cross racing is very different to the road scene because race organisers earn gate money from fans who pay to access these short, closed-circuit courses, with further revenue generated by the sale of broadcast rights, food and drink, and VIP packages. This enables them to pay appearance money to the big names, their presence making it more likely the organiser will make a good return on this investment thanks to a likely boost in the spectator numbers.

In November 2020, Belgian paper *Het Nieuwsblad* revealed that cyclo-cross superstars Mathieu van der Poel and Wout van Aert received €10,000 in appearance fees for racing, apart from in the UCI's World Cup events, where no such payments are made but the prize fund is bigger. Eli Iserbyt was next in the pecking order, with his €2,250 fee less than a quarter of the discipline's two biggest stars. The then Belgian champion Laurens Sweeck and Toon Aerts each received €2,000. During the 2021/22 season, Iserbyt's fee is thought to have tripled thanks to a string of victories leading him to win the World Cup title. Britain's Tom Pidcock is likely to have received a similar amount.

Some of the wheeling and dealing has been removed from this process as a consequence of fees being dependent to some extent on world ranking. The leading three riders in the men's and women's standings are now guaranteed €1,000 per appearance, the next seven riders between €300-€500, with smaller payments for riders below that. The organisers top up these amounts depending on how they view each rider's pulling power.

In the 2021/22 season, the 16-event World Cup series offered the same prize money to men and women. Race winners received €5,000, the 10th-placed riders €1,200, with the prize money stretching down to the 40th rider, who received €300. Series winners Iserbyt and Lucinda Brand each earned €30,000 for their efforts, while the 10th-placed rider took home €6,000 and the 20th-placed €1,000.

STAT ATTACK!
E SPORTS PRIZES

The UCI-sanctioned 2021 World Championships offered a €14,000 prize fund to men and women, the winners of each bagging an equal €8,000 as well as the rainbow jersey to wear for the following year whenever they were competing on the Zwift platform.

"The leading three riders in the men's and women's standings are now guaranteed €1,000 per appearance"

Double U23 CX World Champion Eli Iserbyt is reported to receive appearance money, but not at the same level as the biggest stars Wout van Aert and Mathieu van der Poel

INSTANT EXPERT

PAY GAP NARROWING

Looking at 2021's key numbers the average salary for riders in the (men's) WorldTour, ProTour and Women's WorldTour teams differs significantly.

For WorldTour men it's €402,900, ProTour it's €80,400 and for Women's WorldTour riders it's €61,000. Clearly there is a long way to go to reach parity. However the average salaries are skewed by the biggest stars earning high amounts, and the median rider salary, which reduces that skewing effect, tells a sightly different story.

For WorldTour men it's €170,000, ProTour men it's €46,400 and for Women's WorldTour riders it's €50,000.

GRAVEL RACING STRUCTURE

Like cyclo-cross, the organisers of the leading gravel races have a guaranteed revenue stream that enables them to offer large prize pots to the growing number of professional racers making their living through this fast-developing scene. This comes from the entry fee paid by the hundreds and, in an increasing number of cases, thousands of competitors.

It's the larger races in the USA that the sport's finance is centred around. In 2022, Unbound (previously known as Dirty Kanza) was announced as the flagship event in a six-race gravel and mountain bike series featuring 60 riders and a prize purse of $250,000, the total and number of competitors split equally between men and women. The Belgian Waffle Ride, meanwhile, put up prize money of more than €50,000, once again divided between male and female riders, the winners receiving $5,000 apiece.

As a consequence of the huge and flourishing popularity of gravel racing and associated bikes and equipment, professional road teams are also beginning to add gravel riders to their payroll or to switch road athletes to this discipline. Among the pros who have the full- or part-time move from road to gravel are Peter Stetina, Laurens ten Dam, Lachlan Morton, Alison Tetrick and Andrea Dvorak.

At a glance, the 'double triangle'
shape has lasted 100 years or more,
but under their skin today's pro bikes
are altogether different, as GCN's
Hank discovered filming the 1903
documentary for GCN+

CHAPTER SIX

THE BIKES

From wooden wheel rims to carbon fibre frames, bikes have evolved into today's road racing machines – with variants for CX and gravel

Superficially, the bikes ridden to Tour de France success today are not massively dissimilar to the bike ridden to glory in the first Tour in 1903. They have a 'double-triangle' frame and two wheels, and are powered by pedals and a drivetrain. Look more closely, however, and this simplest of machines has actually evolved almost beyond recognition.

For that inaugural Tour, Maurice Garin's 'La Française' bike featured a steel frame, weighed 18kg, had one gear (reportedly a 52x19), wooden wheel rims and an exciting innovation in the form of toe clips – and he managed to average over 25kph across the race's six stages and 2,428km.

Fast forward to 2021 and Tadej Pogačar rode a one-piece carbon-fibre Colnago V3RS frame, running electronic gearing via Campagnolo's Super Record EPS, with the same manufacturer's carbon wheelset, an SRM power crank and Look Keo Blade clipless pedals. When equipped with disc brakes it weighs 7.1kg, and Pogačar covered the 21 stages and 3,414km at an average speed of over 41kph.

HOW DID WE GET HERE?

Derailleur gear systems were first introduced at the Tour de France in 1937, when Henri Desgranges finally relented on the notion they would make the race too easy. The 1937 Tour winner Roger Lapébie used a rod-actuated Osgear Super Champion rear derailleur. It was at this time that aluminium wheel rims also became the standard, having also previously been against the Tour's draconian rules.

In the following decade gearing progressed with Simplex and Campagnolo introducing front and rear derailleurs, while the latter's Gran Sport cable-operated derailleurs in the 1950s saw manual gear changing become a thing of the past. We had to ›

wait until 2009 for that cable-operated system to be usurped by the introduction of Shimano's electronic groupset, Dura-Ace Di2. In 2011 Cadel Evans became the first rider to win the Tour using electronic shifting, and now all pro road racing bikes run electric groupsets from one manufacturer or another.

A FLOOD OF INNOVATIONS

Steel remained the frame material of choice throughout much of the last century, albeit continually refined and improved, until twin innovations in the use of aluminium and carbon fibre turned bike manufacture on its head. In 1986, Greg LeMond and Bernard Hinault both rode Look's KG86, the first frame made using carbon tubes – with metal lugs – to be ridden at the Tour de France, and LeMond won. Although the use of carbon was undoubtedly a game changer in the long run, metal continued to be the material of choice in the pro peloton with most riders adopting aluminium frames for their comparatively lightweight properties. Marco Pantani completed the last Giro-Tour double as late as 1998 on his aluminium Bianchi Mega Pro XL Reparto Corse.

Look had a more immediate impact with its other major innovation of the era, a 'clip-in' pedal binding system originally developed ❯

LEGENDS OF THE SPORT
GREG LEMOND

The greatest male American cyclist of all time, LeMond was twice World Champion (1983, 1989) and three-times Tour de France winner (1986, 1989, 1990) and has been a motivation and reference point for a generation of riders to follow him. He is a respected and fervent opponent of the use of illegal performance-enhancing drugs by any rider.

INSTANT EXPERT
LOOK KG86

The Look frame, actually built by French aerospace company TVT, introduced Kevlar to the carbon fibre tubes to improve stiffness and handling, and these tubes then met at aluminium lugs while the frame and fork also featured metal dropouts. Both riding the KG86 in the 1986 Tour de France Greg LeMond beat his La Vie Claire teammate Bernard Hinault on GC.

PRO'S PERSPECTIVE

ADVANCES IN AERODYNAMICS

*Six-time Italian TT champion **Marco Pinotti** on how technology is winning the battle against air resistance*

"As someone whose focus has been very much on time trials, I'm not that surprised by the improvements in this technology over the past 15 years. It's an important issue because riders can now feel the difference when it comes to the aerodynamics of road bikes. Before, it was considered important with regard to time trial equipment, but now it's just as vital with road bikes. People want a faster skinsuit, a fast helmet and, of course, a fast bike. Most brands now offer a more aerodynamic road bike, with deep-section wheels, and that's making the pro peloton faster.

"What impact it can have depends on how you race. If you have to pull on the front of the bunch or if you go in the breakaway, then it's become extremely important; the aerodynamics are effectively giving you a little bit more power. If you're sitting in the bunch on the wheel, then there's less effect, but you still save energy if you're in the peloton on an aero bike.

"Switching to a more aerodynamic bike can make a team more competitive. It's the little details that can make a big difference, especially if you bear in mind the UCI has kept the permitted minimum weight of bikes to 6.8kg. As materials have got better and, at the same time, so has the knowledge of how to use them, bikes can be shaped in a different way and still remain at or very close to 6.8kg. Manufacturers can work the frame a little more, make adjustments after testing with the rider in the wind tunnel – not just with the bike on its own. Small things that they can see make a difference because they can measure them."

PInotti acknowledges that there is also a psychological aspect. "If a rider believes a bike is faster, they will often ride faster. Sometimes you'll see a team switch to a new supplier and start getting better results. There's probably some good science behind that improvement, but there's probably also a bit of a placebo effect, too, that comes from simply believing they're going to race faster."

HOW NEW TECH CHANGES RACE ACTION

How the major technological developments affect riding, tactics and, ultimately, the fan's experience

Aero Frames

Initially, carbon fibre bike frames — and then components — were for weight saving, but with the UCI introducing a minimum bike weight limit, attention turned to carbon's manipulability. It's possible to shape tubes quite radically without the sort of weight penalty that the same process with metal would incur. As a result even the lightest climbing bikes have adapted technology from TT bikes to become more aerodynamic, saving watts at speeds as low as 20kph, allowing riders to compete fresher and hopefully faster at the top of summit finishes or in flat stage sprints.

Disc Brakes

Still an area of contention, despite now being used in the vast majority of races, discs have made a significant difference to braking distances and enabled riders to descend faster and react later. While this has led to more of the racing being full gas, there are those in the peloton who feel the increased control given by the brakes has led to more risks being taken and more crashes as a result. It was a point made by Romain Bardet after Julian Alaphilippe's horror crash at the 2022 Liège-Bastogne-Liège, but the technology is here to stay and the riders will no doubt adapt.

Dropper Seatposts

Although allowed in road racing for some years by the UCI — in part to aid neutral service vehicles providing bikes to fit a variety of riders — Matej Mohorič's use of a dropper post to descend to victory at the 2022 Milano-Sanremo was a revelation. Mohorič's tactic was a tried and tested one, with Sean Kelly having famously used a daring descent from the race's final climb to overhaul Moreno Argentin in 1992, but the Slovenian insisted that lowering his saddle height with the dropper post had improved his handling and control of his bike and enabled him to take risks that the riders still with him at the top of the climb just could not match. We're almost certain to see more dropper posts at future editions of Milano-Sanremo, and perhaps several Grand Tour stages given the current trend for fewer summit finishes on mountain stages.

Unwelcome in cycling since revelations of his cheating emerged, it was Lance Armstrong who rode the first monocoque carbon frame in the Tour de France

Stephen Roche, the last rider to win the Tour de France in toe clips, before clipless systems became ubiquitous

for skiing. Launched in 1984, the first Look clipless pedal spawned development from other brands. The toe clip was soon dead; Stephen Roche, in 1987, was the last Tour winner to use them.

WEIGHTIER MATTERS

Since a certain Lance Armstrong returned to racing in 1999 aboard a Trek 5500, which introduced super-light full monocoque carbon construction and was the first fully carbon bike to 'win' the Tour de France (Armstrong's record subsequently expunged due to his cheating), every Tour-winning bike thereafter has followed suit. The current UCI 6.8kg minimum weight was introduced in 2000, however, and with weight becoming a level playing field, manufacturers at the very top end have been chasing aerodynamic gains ever since. The then-radical Cervélo Soloist in 2001 can claim to be the first truly aero road bike, as opposed to a track or time trial bike, some of which had adopted highly radical design elements until the UCI once again stepped in. Wind tunnel research has continued, producing bikes such as the Specialized Venge for Mark Cavendish made in conjunction with McLaren, using the F1 team's experience with composite technology and aerodynamics.

The introduction of disc brakes may have done the most to change the look of the road bike. After early controversy, they are now commonplace in the pro peloton where they improve braking performance and can help a superlight frame reach the 6.8kg limit. Tour champion Tadej Pogačar often switches between disc and rim brakes depending on the parcours, although he seems to be one of the last advocates for rim brakes in the pro peloton. ❯

176cm tall, Tadej Pogačar rode a size 50s Colnago V3RS to back-to-back Tour de France victories

POGAČAR'S TOUR WINNING BIKE

The whole pro peloton ride well designed and spec'd bikes, and the winner of 2021's biggest race rode this Colnago V3RS

SADDLE
Tadej Pogačar uses a Prologo Scratch M5 saddle with carbon fibre rail

FRAME
The V3RS has a monocoque carbon frame to chase the optimum balance of lightness and aerodynamic performance

BRAKES
On flat courses and hilly yet fast parcours Pogačar uses discs, but on a climb the rim brake option saves 300g

DRIVETRAIN
Campagnolo SR 54/39 chainrings, 11-32 cassette, 172.5mm crank arms – equipped with an SRM power meter

COCKPIT
The carbon fibre Deda Alanera monocoque handlebar is 38cm wide with a 120mm long stem

WHEELSET
When using disc brakes it's the Bora Ultra WTO with tubeless tyres. On rim brakes Pogačar uses the Bora Ultra 50 with tubulars

FORK
The fork has aerodynamic curved blades in the upper portion, and more clearance for tyres up to 28mm

PRO'S PERSPECTIVE
POGAČAR'S MECHANIC

UAE Team Emirates' Giuseppe Archetti is the mechanic with the answers!

What's most important about preparing a bike for a Grand Tour leader and winner?

Before a big tour an extraordinary maintenance is done to make sure that the bicycles are also in the best condition to face a very tough competition. One particular request from Tadej is that he prefers to ride with relatively low tyre pressures.

How many of you work on the bikes during a Grand Tour?

There are four mechanics: in rotation two of us are in the team car and two stay at the hotel to prepare for the next day. Normally the day starts at 7am and closes at 9-9.30pm.

How difficult is it to prepare for different stages?

The stages with a lot of climbing are the ones that challenge us most because we have to change the ratios of the bicycle both front and rear. As for the rear cassette it is faster while it is more demanding if we have to change the front chainrings. Weather conditions can also cause changes in tyre pressure. If the road is wet, the pressure must be lower than when the road is dry. For the TT there are no big differences because the bikes are already set to the riders' specifications.

How similar are the pro's bikes to the ones the public can buy?

There are no differences because the material we use must be available for sale. ❯

SADDLE
Elisa Balsamo rides with a Bontrager Aeolus Pro Saddle

ELISA BALSAMO'S WC EMONDO BIKE

Classics set-up is a little different to GC. Here's the Trek bike that the women's' World Champion raced at the 2022 Ronde van Vlaanderen

FRAME
52cm Trek Emonda SLR800 World Champions Disc frame and fork. Total bike weight: 6.95kg

GEARING
SRAM 10-33 cassette paired with SRAM 50/37 Powermeter Chainring

GROUPSET
SRAM Red eTap AXS disc brake groupset with an extra four wireless shifters, and Ceramic BB

COCKPIT
Bontrager RSL one-piece bar & stem. 38x100 with -7° angle, and Wahoo Elemnt Bolt computer

WHEELSET
Bontrager Aeolus RSL 51 wheels with Pirelli PZero Race TLR 28mm tubeless tyres: 4.1bar front, 4.3 rear

BEARINGS
Trek-Segafredo use Kogel wheel bearings on Elisa Balsamo's bike

PRO'S PERSPECTIVE
BALSAMO'S MECHANIC

Trek Segafredo's Team Support Manager (and former mechanic) Glen Leven shares the inside view

What's most important about preparing a bike for a Classics leader?

For any race, but especially the Classics, every detail counts for the complete team.

A leader's bike is, of course, special and you need to pay close attention to it. We double check with them to see if they want to have the set-up as previous races etc, and make any adjustments necessary. The important thing is that they feel confident and happy with their bike head of the race.

How many of you work on the team's bikes at the Classics?

During the Classics, the hardest part is preparing the bikes and we have three mechanics who are dedicated to doing this. We are riding different tyres, different handlebar set-ups, and this takes time to build. Normally you need just one day, for the Classics you need three full days with three mechanics.

How do you adapt the bike to cope with different surfaces?

The most important change is often the tyres. For Strade Bianche, our riders were racing on their normal bike with 20mm Pirelli tyres, for Flanders, we have a Classics set-up with some riders changing bars, using double bar tape and tyres with less pressure. For Roubaix, it's a completely different bike with different tyres again, 30mm tubeless with inserts. ❯

SADDLE
Ganna's Fizik Ares saddle features grip tape in the nose to help him maintain position as far forward as possible

FILIPPO GANNA'S PINARELLO

The reigning TT World Champion used this stunning Pinarello F12 X Light to win the first and last stages of the 2021 Giro d'Italia

FRAME
The chrome blue frame and fork is extensively shaped and contoured all over to reduce drag

GEARING
Rear gearing features an 11-30T cassette and a long-cage aluminium rear mech from an Ultegra groupset

CHAINSET
Ganna delivers his awesome power via a Shimano Dura-Ace Di2 9100 crankset with massive 58/46 chainrings

COCKPIT
One-piece custom carbon base bar and stem with extensions moulded to fit Ganna's forearms

BRAKES
Rim brake callipers are integrated into the frame and covered with fairings to aid airflow while meeting UCI regulations

WHEELSET
Ganna uses a Princeton Carbon Works Rear Disc Wheel and AeroCoach 100mm front wheel

INSTANT EXPERT
TIME TRIAL BIKE CHOICES

There are no rules that state a TT must be ridden on a TT bike, and sometimes bits of them aren't, so why do riders swap bikes on a TT?

Vast sums are spent designing aerodynamic bikes for time trials, so why would the pros ditch them for a regular road bike as both Tadej Pogačar and Primož Roglič did in the stage 20 TT that decided the 2020 Tour de France?

Usually, they don't. Aero gains outweigh weight gains at speeds over 20kph, and no pro rides anywhere near as slow as that... except for when the organisers choose to finish with an ascent.

A rider and DS will calculate whether the time savings of riding a steep climb on a lighter road bike outweigh the time lost to the bike swap (assuming it goes well!). This depends on the type of rider as well as the course.

If the team decides to go for it, the swap will take place at a pre-agreed location on the course, with the rider slowing to a halt as the mechanic climbs out of the car, jumping on the road bike and getting a push to get back up to speed. A good organised swap can take less than 10 seconds.

At the 2017 UCI World Championships in Bergen, Norway, the organisers even created a specific bike change zone ahead of the finishing climb, but while Primož Roglič switched bikes to finish second, winner Tom Dumoulin rode his TT bike throughout. ❯

GRAVEL BIKE ANATOMY & SET-UP

*Former road pro turned gravel specialist **Peter Stetina** on what makes a winning gravel bike*

PRO'S PERSPECTIVE

ROAD VS CX BIKE SETUP
Lucinda Brand

>> "Gravel is its own discipline now, the fastest growing one in the sport. The bikes are most similar to a cyclo-cross bike. However, while cyclo-cross bikes are more upright, have higher bottom brackets, are twitchy, gravel bikes are more slacked out, built for higher speeds on rougher roads. It's all about compliance while still having something of a road geometry, but with an emphasis on tyre clearance, wider tyres, flare bars that come out at like a 15-to 20-degree angle — the latter useful for bar bags and better handling.

"While in cyclo-cross it's about mud clearance and tyres are really thin, they're much wider in gravel — 40mm is the happy medium — and there'll be some light knob on them making your gravel bike a go-anywhere, do-anything bike. For every race, I change my gear and especially my tyre combinations — the tyres are the biggest things that change, day to day even. I'd say that I've sealed more tyres in two years than during my whole life previously. Tyre pressure varies a lot. It's all about dialling all those details in.

"Gravel racing is a lot about damage control — not *if*, necessarily, but *when* and how badly you puncture, so tyre sealant choices are important, as is quick access to plugs and things, so maybe you don't stash them away in your seat bag, but have them in your pocket where the gels would usually be. You have to think about fixing on the fly — it's very much a self-supported ethos. While there are races that have aid stations, you have to be ready to mitigate disaster at a moment's notice.

"One other thing I'm really particular about is the split seatpost on Canyon's gravel bikes, that have a slot down the middle. It is amazing for rough roads, and if I were to go back into the WorldTour, I would use that at anything like Strade Bianche or Roubaix. I know roadies all like the stiff and hard ride, but this post can make such a difference, it's amazing."

"The biggest difference between my road bike and my 'cross bike is the set-up of my steerer. My set-up is designed for me to be a bit shorter and a little bit higher on the bike, and also my handlebar is one size bigger. If you compare it to a mountain bike bar, it's really wide, so you can deal with really tight corners and have a bit more control over my bike. Going a little wider with my bars helps to make sure that my technique is better."

"You have to think about fixing on the fly — gravel biking is very much a self-supported ethos"

PETER STETINA'S CANYON GRIZL

The 2021 Belgian Waffle Ride Utah-winning bike has wide tyres, stacks of mud clearance, bult-in power-meter and a desert-themed paint-job

COCKPIT
The PRO Discover carbon bar has a 20-degree flare designed to work with Shimano GRX 815 Di2 shifters

WHEELSET
42c IRC Boken Doublecross tyres on Shimano Dura-Ace R9170 C40 Tubeless wheels with GRX RX810 brakes

DRIVETRAIN
Shimano Dura-Ace R9100-P with dual-sided power meter, 50/36 chainrings and 11-34 cassette

Amongst the numerous former road pro's tempted by gravel, GCN's own Si Richardson raced Colorado's Steamboat Epic

GRAVEL VS CX SETUP
Hannah Otto

"Gravel bikes have a shorter reach and a lower bottom bracket to lower that centre of gravity, in 'cross, you need the higher bottom bracket for cornering and to clear obstacles. It's going to be less racy, so it'll have less aggressive geometry because on the gravel bike you're going to be on it all day long, potentially.

You might also have something like an Iso Flex seatpost to help dampen some of the bumps. You also probably have wider tyres; I gravitate towards a 40-42c tyre."

CHAPTER SEVEN

HOW RACES ARE WON

The parcours of a stage or race dictates the tactics a team will adopt. But with so many different factors to juggle and opportunities to explore it's a game of cunning and subterfuge, based on strategies for success

>> Strategy and preparation have long been important in deciding how to approach a race. In their different forms, data and tech play an increasing role, along with continued reliance on good old-fashioned DS and rider instinct.

From the outside, and especially to those who are new to the sport, road racing can look formulaic, with a typical stage unfolding like this: the peloton rolls away, the break forms, the break gains a gap, the peloton chases/doesn't chase, the break is reeled in/goes the distance, the peloton contests the sprint/ a small group contests the sprint/one rider wins alone. This is essentially the framework, but within it all manner of strategies, tactics and manoeuvres are cooked up and enacted by up to 25 rival teams. At the same time as these are having an impact on the shape of the race, the riders also must prepare to react to changes in the race conditions – the wind picking up from a certain direction, for instance, or a crash that leaves team leaders stranded for a brief time or even puts them out of the race completely.

Like a mini weather system travelling across the countryside, the shape, speed and mood of the peloton are constantly changing. Understanding how and why that happens enhances the viewing experience immensely... ›

Whether it's by the smallest margin in a photo finish or a day-long solo break, a victory is what riders and team directors plan for

Anna Kiesenhofer's strategy at the Tokyo 2020 Olympic Games worked well: get in the break then TT to the finish! This time the Dutch-led chasing group didn't get it right

Unknown unknowns: Tour de France race boss Christian Prudhomme explains to Egan Bernal why the Extreme Weather Protocol was invoked in the 2019 race

SETTING A STRATEGY

Working out how a day's racing is likely to pan out and setting a strategy for it is a skill that demands a combination of innate insight and experience. It's a task that divides into two parts. Firstly, there are what would be described in Rumsfeldian style as the 'known knowns'. These can be highlighted and prepared for in the pre-race/stage analysis – the number, location and difficulty of the climbs, for instance, or the places where the wind might have an impact on the action, or the pinch points that might be an obstacle due to road furniture, a sharp bend or a narrowing of the road itself.

Then, there are 'known unknowns', those factors that emerge during the course of an event that might require tactical adjustments, a key rider crashing, perhaps, or revealing that their form is not at its best and that another teammate should be given the opportunity to lead. Bearing in mind that bike racing takes place on public roads where fans, the elements and other factors can all influence the nature of the action, there's always the possibility of 'unknown unknowns' arising: rare or even unprecedented incidents that can have a dramatic bearing on how the action unfolds. One example of this would be the opening stage of the 2021 Tour de France, when a careless spectator stepped in front of the bunch brandishing a sign

"There's always the possibility of 'unknown unknowns' arising, having a bearing on how the action unfolds"

displaying a message to her grandparents. Team directors, their road captains and the individual riders couldn't have predicted this but have to be prepared for everything and to be aware of the constant ebbs and flows within a race, constantly calculating where a team's riders need to be in order to ensure that the day's objectives can be achieved.

UNDERSTANDING PARCOURS

Although there are instances of leading riders being as successful in a new role as team directors at the end of their competitive career, Italy's inter-war cycling legend Alfredo Binda being a prime example of this phenomenon, the best team directors often had support roles within teams when they were racing, acting as a road captain perhaps, depending on ability to read a race, their **>**

💬
JARGON BUSTER
PARCOURS

From the French, literally for 'journey', in cycling *parcours* means the course itself, the route that the race or stage takes, including length, elevation, steepness and technical difficulty of climbs and descents.

quickness of thought enabling them to compete on a level playing field with riders who had a physical advantage over them.

BikeExchange-Jayco DS Matt White is a good example of a solid ex-pro who was prized for his qualities as a road captain, and who has gone on to achieve more success as a directeur sportif. For the Australian, pre-race analysis and planning comprises a number of phases and is more like chess than poker…

"Obviously, the preparation for a one-day race, compared to a stage race and compared to a three-week tour can vary," explains White. "In a three-week tour, you're thinking of the long game, whereas in one-day races it's a different mentality – you're using different riders in different roles in a different way, because there's no tomorrow in a one-day race. You've also got to adapt those strategies around your leaders. Certain leaders have certain styles, they have a way that they like to ride, and you've got to work those preferences into your plans.

BAROUDEUR

A French term loosely translating as 'adventurer' and applied breakaway specialists. Some attack knowing that their effort is doomed, but that they'll spend time in front of the TV cameras, which the team's sponsors will be happy about. Others, such as Belgian Thomas De Gendt and Italian Alessandro De Marchi, make a career from searching out stage-winning opportunities.

"In a three-week tour, you're thinking of the long game, whereas in one-day races it's a different mentality"

"I understand that people see strategy as being a bit of a gamble, that there's an element of poker playing in it. But what you've got to remember is that, especially when it comes to stage racing, when you decide on a tactic you're not the only person or team with that goal or tactic. Sometimes you do gamble a little bit that someone else might take up the pace-making or the pursuit of a group before you do, or you might be gambling that someone else will come and help you with that tactic, so there is a degree of that involved. But you've also got to have your strategy, based on the outcome that you've got to work towards. Sometimes that means you just have to step up and make those decisions before someone else does.

"Working out strategy is becoming more complex all the time. We've got a lot of technology these days such as GPX files and various mapping apps that enable us to see the routes on a screen and we can certainly get a good gauge of how they are. Personally, I also like to get a visual idea of them by doing recons. You can get a clearer impression of how the race might pan out. Some of those stages might not even be days when the race is won, but you can get a very good idea of how to save energy on those days by seeing the terrain in person. Then you've got other stages where, for instance, if you've got a ❯

LEGENDS OF THE SPORT
CONNIE CARPENTER-PHINNEY

The USA's Connie Carpenter became a 'legend' by winning the road race at the 1984 Los Angeles Olympics on a bike throw from fellow American Rebecca Twigg, on the same day the men's race was won by USA's Alexi Grewal. But this was no flash-in-the-pan; she won 12 national titles on road and track, and twice podiumed in the road World Championships.

Unforeseen incidents can ruin your strategy in a split second. The 2021 Tour de France saw two large crashes on stage 1; with nerves high, the early days of a Grand Tour are dangerous

Some roads are known, for others Google Maps helps, but they all need a proper recce pre-race

Knowing all the bends and road furniture is vital in planning a sprint lead-out. Here Trek-Segafredo got Lizzie Deignan set up for the win

Team BikeExchange-Jayco DS Matt White briefs his riders pre-race, primarily on how to look after Simon Yates, but has to be ready to change plans on the fly

sprinter on a team you have to do a different kind of research. You can look at a final for a sprint stage, but it's not going to look anything like that on the day of the stage. You're not going to see how they're going to barricade out the final kilometres. You don't know what road furniture they're going to remove when you see a stage three months beforehand...

"Even after you do paint a mental picture of how you think a stage will pan out, you still have to be flexible in your strategy because if something big happens the day before that upturns the applecart on the GC front, then that stage won't evolve as you expected and you've obviously got to adapt to a whole new situation. Ultimately, all of the planning comes together in the pre-race briefing you give on the team

> ### "Even after painting a mental picture of how a stage will pan out, you still have to be flexible in your strategy"

bus. They've changed massively since I was racing. It's like the difference between night and day. If you'd told me 15 years ago that I'd be giving PowerPoint presentations, daily, for a simple road stage, I would have scoffed. But now I'm doing it. That kind of technology wasn't available 15 years ago when I first started. All you had was a road book and they were pretty basic. It might have some pictures that were sometimes a little bit dubious, ❯

Milano-Sanremo often comes down to a sprint, but typically in small numbers. Julian Alaphilippe won in 2019 but couldn't hold off Wout van Aert in 2020

and if you were lucky you might have a diagram of the last 3km. Some old-school directors used to get maps out and they could tell what kind of roads they were, if they were B-roads, national highways or smaller country roads. Teams didn't really do recons, per se, because you couldn't get the information you needed about where the route was going to go. Obviously, in the mountains, you could work it out, but nearer to towns it was impossible. That's all changed massively. We can see every bit of the route now, the tricky corners, the gradient. The key now is to filter all of the information you have access to so that the riders receive the most important details."

ONE-DAY RACES: THRILLERS

While stage races are cycling's soap operas, the story unfolding over several days to reach what should be a dramatic climax, one-day races are the sport's thrillers, where everything's on the

SANREMO SPRINT?

It's a common misconception that Milano-Sanremo is a 300km race which ends in a bunch sprint. Over the past 30 years, the average size of the group at the finish is 17.6. We haven't had a group larger than 10 since 2016 (31 riders) when Arnaud Démare won, and for Alexander Kristoff's victory in 2014 it was still only 25. Hardly 'bunch sprints'!

In one-day races planned attacks stretch the peloton towards breaking point...

...until a reduced bunch of the best riders is ready to compete for the win

INSTANT EXPERT

RACE DISTANCE

UCI's maximum distances for Elite Men one-day races

300km
WorldTour Races

250-280km
Olympic Games and World Championships

240km
Continental Championships, Continental Games, Regional Championships, National Championships

200km
Continental 1.HC and 1.1
(can be extended by UCI committee)
Continental 1.2
(no chance to extend)

100km
WorldTour TTT stage max distance

80km
WorldTour ITT stage max distance

 JARGON BUSTER

THE BUNCH

Also more commonly known by the French term *peloton*, the bunch is the main group of riders.

line and anything can happen. The initial scenario for a one-day race is fundamentally the same as for a stage on a multi-day event – a break forms, opens a lead, then the chase begins. Yet, while the break is likely to maintain its cohesion, because there's more chance of them going the distance if they can keep their numbers together for as long as possible, the peloton tends to go through a whittling-down process that will leave the strongest riders at the front. This shake-out might happen on the cobbles of Roubaix, the bergs of Flanders, the hills of Liège... At the same time, the break will be reeled in inexorably.

The beauty of the finale of a one-day race is that it tends to pit individuals against each other, producing an unpredictable contest where alliances are quickly formed and just as quickly liquidated, and where strength, tactical nous and a good finishing kick will pay dividends. (See more on p214.)

A Grand Tour GC leader's jersey is a source of great pride, not least for the Spaniard Jesus Herrada, wearing the Vuelta's red jersey, in 2018

Bunch sprint finishes are high intensity action for fans, with the 'trains' working from a script but always prepared to ad-lib. Here Elisa Balsamo, in white, got it right at Gent-Wevelgem 2022

PROLOGUE

A short first day of competitive riding, usually an ITT, in a stage race with a distance too short to be considered a full stage, typically 9km or less. They showcase riders and teams, establish early gaps and initial jersey holders and set the scene for Stage 1.

As David Millar – multiple stage winner in all three Grand Tours – advises in his CHPT3 blog: "Starting fast in a prologue is imperative – there's no riding into it and finding your rhythm, as is the norm in a time trial."

INSTANT EXPERT
WORLD TOUR STAGE DISTANCES

Race organisers have room to be creative with their craft – for sporting challenge, entertainment and logistics – but there are some limitations to stage length, including:

240km
Max stage distance

180km
Average daily distance

60km
ITT / TTT max stage distance

STAGE RACES: STRUCTURED FOR STRATEGY

Designed by organisers to create the best challenges for competitors and the most exciting spectacles for fans – roadside or via broadcast – the types of stages, their severity and their order demand a lot of planning

As we explored in Chapter 3, these are multi-day events, from as short as two days in length up to three-week Grand Tours. The most prestigious prize goes to the winner of the general classification; the rider who completes all of a race's stages in the lowest cumulative time. This competition's leader wears a distinctive jersey – yellow in the Tour de France and in the many races that follow its precedent, pink in the Giro d'Italia, red in the Vuelta a España, yellow and blue in the Critérium du Dauphiné and green and white in the Volta a Catalunya.

As well as the overall title, stage races feature a number of other competitions, notably the points classification for the most consistent rider in terms of finishing position; the mountains classification for the best climber; the best young rider's classification; the team classification; and the intermediate sprints classification, although in some races, most notably the Tour, this latter prize has been rolled into the points competition. In short, stage races are about much more than who wins on any one day or who takes the overall victory in the end. This heightens the strategic and tactical essence of stage races considerably.

TYPES OF STAGE
Road-race stages essentially break down into four categories: sprint, mountain, individual time trial (ITT) and team time trial (TTT).

SPRINT STAGES ARE GENERALLY FLAT OR ROLLING
On terrain of this kind, the riders within the peloton are usually very equally matched. In other words, it's difficult for individual riders or individual teams to gain a significant advantage over their rivals. Sprint stages tend to be the most formulaic. In most cases, a small group of breakaway riders will ride clear in the opening kilometres and the peloton will then set about keeping them within a respectable distance. This suits both the escapees and the bunch rolling along them behind, firstly by giving the

Riders from smaller teams try to get in the breakaway, 'rolling the dice' for success, and making themselves, and their sponsors' logos, visible. Here, it worked, as Damiano Cima of Nippo Vini Fantini Faizane won stage 18 of the 2019 Giro d'Italia

former the sniff of a stage victory and, often more importantly, allowing the teams involved to show off their sponsors' logos and brands in the full focus on the TV cameras, and secondly by closing down the likelihood of further attacks from the peloton.

As a consequence, a familiar scenario unfolds, the break extending its advantage to reach a margin that's pre-established by the directors of the sprinters' teams in their pre-stage briefing. Once the escapees have opened a gap of, say, five minutes, the sprinters' teams, often with the collaboration of the team that's defending the leader's jersey, will set a pace on the front of the peloton to match that of the break. Then, at another pre-decided point, the teams leading the peloton will gradually increase its speed, steadily reeling in the breakaway before it reaches the finish, before setting up their sprinters for the eyeballs-out sprint that will decide the day's spoils.

Occasionally the break will go the distance, either because the peloton has got its calculations wrong or, particularly in the final week of Grand Tours, because the sprinters' teams no longer have the firepower to commit to the chase. The possibility of this scenario unfolding tempts a few hopefuls into the break. (See more on stage race and breakaway tactics on p216-220.) ❯

INSTANT EXPERT
CATCHING THE BREAKAWAY

So the breakaway is *usually* caught, but how do the chasers work it out? Neutral services vehicles share the status, typically motos with a chalkboard. In-car Directeur Sportifs talk via radio with their riders and road captains, both in the break and in the chasing group, calculating how and when to catch the break to make the best of their strategy.

A rule of thumb – voiced by 1950s French pro Robert Chapatte, and thus known as Chapatte's law – is that the peloton will close down the break at around 1 minute per 10km. Terrain, tiredness and especially each group's willingness to work together affects this ratio.

While Arnaud De Lie started 2022 well, claiming the Volta Limburg Classic, his mentor Caleb Ewan was bossing the Tour des Alpes

PRO'S PERSPECTIVE

SPRINT FINISHES

*Lotto-Soudal DS **Cherie Pridham** outlines tactics for sprint stages with experienced and neo-pro sprinters*

Cherie Pridham

A pro rider for 15 years, competing at the top level, Pridham moved into management with Team Raleigh and Vitus Pro Cycling. She became the first female DS on the men's WorldTour with Israel Start-Up Nation (where she was the first female DS to win a WT stage, with Mads Würtz Schmidt at Tirreno-Adriatico, 2021), before joining Lotto-Soudal.

"For Arnaud De Lie, all our work would be in protecting him, making sure he was in a good position. We'd always have somebody with him, a rider, maybe two, during the race, and then it'd be all in for good positioning, into the roundabouts, or left and right turns. Riders would be well drilled as to what the profile is, they'd be aware of each kilometre, and they'll have a Google Earth overview of the final 5km. Then it's really down to how we structure which rider does the final run-in, so whether that's the last man peeling off at 500 to go depending on the parcours, who rides the final km and how they line up in front of Arnaud. It's very much down to communication as well, to laying out a plan and making sure that the riders understand it. Then it's down to them.

"If the sprint is uphill or technical, lead-out riders will be working until closer to the line or to a corner that's particularly important. Caleb Ewan is very adaptable in these finishes and can deal with almost anything. When it comes to Arnaud, we call him our little bull. He's really showing that he can do all sorts as well... It's all about horses and courses. Caleb is obviously very experienced. He will know how to talk with these riders and what to expect. If it were a stage where Caleb was the protected leader, a lot of discussion will be done in the meeting in the bus. Whereas, sometimes when you have a younger sprinter, it's about them learning on the road as well. Essentially, almost as much as the nature of the finish, it's the degree of experience that influences strategy in sprints."

The Tour of the Alps presents climbing and mountain finish opportunities for the likes of Team DSM's Romain Bardet

GC MOUNTAIN FINISH

*Team DSM Directeur Sportif **Luke Roberts** considers mountain-top and valley stage finishes when outlining strategies for General Classification*

"When you're building strategy around a GC leader, you have to look at his qualities, know where you can gain time with him, where he's going to be vulnerable and where he needs looking after. Once you've pinned down that overall strategy, you can look at specific stages and obviously the days in the mountains will be a key part of that.

"If we're in a Grand Tour and targeting the GC, we'll pick out the stages that we think are the key ones. We analyse which are the stages where you might be able to make the difference where people might be not expecting it. You also have to look at how you can manage the energy of your entire team so that they can get through those three weeks, work out the days where they can take it a bit easier, the days where if they race hard they'll also be able to put a bit of pressure on everybody else, as well as thinking about when to expect other teams to put pressure on. You want to establish how you potentially make good things happen for your team, but also be prepared for what might get thrown at you."

Luke Roberts
An Olympic gold medalist, World Champion and world record holder in track Team Pursuit, Aussie Roberts was a road racing pro for more than a decade, and includes the mountains classification (and top 10 GC) at the 2011 Tour Down Under on his palmarès.

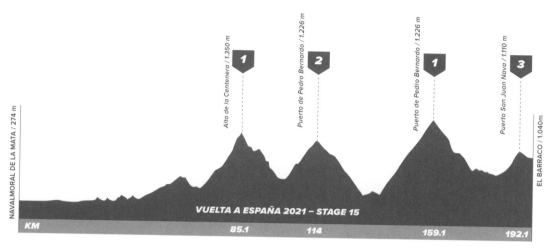

VUELTA A ESPAÑA 2021 – STAGE 15

NAVALMORAL DE LA MATA / 274 m

Alto de la Centenera / 1.350 m — **1**

Puerto de Pedro Bernardo / 1.226 m — **2**

Puerto de Pedro Bernardo / 1.226 m — **1**

Puerto San Juan Nava / 1.110 m — **3**

EL BARRACO / 1.040m

KM   85.1   114   159.1   192.1

SIMON'S VIEW
MEASURING MOUNTAINS

In road cycling, mountains are classified based on increasing difficulty, from category 4 to *hors categorie*. These categories are defined by their steepness, length and where they're located on the stage. A category-1 climb, for example, could be elevated to *hors categorie* status if it's the final ascent of the day where the riders will already be drenched in fatigue.

That's the rather banal factual explanation anyway. Legend has it – and legend is always more interesting than reality – that categories are based on the gear a Citroën 2CV would use to reach the summit. So, fourth gear for a cat-4, third gear for a cat-3 and so on. When it came to the *hors categorie*, that was deemed beyond categorisation and reserved for ascents that the 2CV simply couldn't climb.

MOUNTAIN STAGES, BIG AND SMALL

Although the description 'mountain stage' suggests climbs passing beneath lofty, snow-capped peaks, there's a range of stages that fall within this category. They may feature a series of smaller climbs that are typically described as 'medium mountain', from the French *moyenne montagne*. Higher mountain stages are precisely that, often featuring a summit finish. In essence, the basic racing scenario is the same as the sprint stages. A breakaway group forms, the peloton allows them some leeway, then a chase usually begins, led by the teams aiming for the overall title or at least a place well up in the standings.

Breakaways on mountain stages are much more likely to go the distance because the riders that join them tend to be out of the running for the overall title and are focusing their efforts on the mountains jersey or on that individual stage. The GC contenders, meanwhile, are primarily focused on each other and on their own energy reserves. As a result, they are less inclined to chase down a breakaway group unless the escapees are well within range. Otherwise, it's not expedient to devote the resources to do so, because this will come at a cost later in the race.

INDIVIDUAL TIME TRIALS

Individual time trials – ITT – include prologue time trials that get a stage race under way and can be as short as a kilometre in length, rising to a maximum of 8km. Any individual test above this length is classified as a time trial and these can extend to as much as 80km. While tests of this duration weren't uncommon two or three decades ago, most time trials nowadays fall within a range of 10 to 40 kilometres.

The riders set off, usually at one-minute intervals, in reverse order of general classification, so the rider in last place is the first to   ❯

Under the Nice sun at the 2013 Tour de France, Orica-GreenEDGE's negative split TTT saw them overhaul Omega Pharma-QuickStep's 3-sec advantage at the halfway point

start and the rider in the leader's jersey goes off last knowing exactly what time they have to achieve in order to retain the lead. When overtaking or being overtaken, drafting isn't allowed.

TEAM TIME TRIALS

Team time trials – TTT – take place during the first third of a stage race. So, during a Grand Tour, they're scheduled during the opening week, when teams will have sufficient riders to cope with the demands of this spectacular test. Teams start in reverse order based on their position in the team classification, but with the race leader's team going off last. In a Grand Tour featuring eight-rider line-ups, each team's time is taken when the fifth rider crosses the line, a stipulation that's designed to encourage cooperation between riders whose strengths vary considerably. If, for instance, a team includes four rouleurs and four climbers, the former, who are stronger on the flat, will do longer turns on the front of the line than the latter, which not only ensures a faster overall speed, but also makes it more likely that the climbers, or at the very least one of them, will be able to stay with the rouleurs' pace.

At the finish, teams are credited with the time of the fifth rider across the line. Any riders that have been dropped have to finish the test and within a cut-off point that's equivalent to the winning team's time plus 25%. ❯

TOUR'S FASTEST TT

The fastest team time trial in Tour de France history is an average **57.84km/hr**, generated by **Orica-GreenEDGE** in 2013. **Rohan Dennis** holds the mantle as fastest individual time triallist, registering an average **55.45km/hr** during stage 1 of the 2015 Tour.

A successful track rider turned roadie, Rohan Dennis defended his UCI ITT title at the 2019 World Championships in Yorkshire, wearing his Australian national colours

RACE STRATEGY: 'CHESS ON WHEELS'

Often described as 'chess on wheels' road racing's strategic demands are bewilderingly complex

>> Perhaps this complexity isn't that surprising when you consider that up to 25 teams are pitted against each other in open terrain where the weather can have a significant impact and where ill luck, such as a crash or a mechanical, can occur at any moment. In short, no one can have a precise idea of what will happen, which means that tactical knowledge, racing experience and the ability to 'read' a race are premium attributes for both riders and team directors if success is to be achieved.

RIDING IN THE BUNCH

This is the most fundamental skill for any road racer because every single one of them will spend the majority of their time within the peloton due to the energy-saving advantage that it presents. Watching on TV or from the roadside, sitting in the wheels within the bunch can look easy. Look a little closer, though, and especially at overhead images of the peloton, and the skill levels required become much more apparent, particularly when the race is on and the peloton is moving at high speed. At these points, the peloton resembles a living organism, pulsating constantly, broadening in size on wide stretches of road or when its speed eases off, compacting and stretching when the road narrows or the pace rises.

Once the race is on, the peloton has a peculiar circulatory system. Each rider has to fight for their place on the road, even if they want to hold their position within the bunch. That's because a lot of the riders behind them will be attempting to move closer to the front, jinking through tiny gaps just ahead of them, rubbing elbows and shoulders as they do so, knocking the handlebars on either side to create a space, always looking for the next gap to emerge. Yet, most of these riders won't want to reach the very front of the bunch, but just be within reach of it when the moment arrives when they'll need to put their nose in the wind, perhaps to protect their GC leader or to lead out their sprinter.

When, in the midst of this washing machine-like process, most of the riders on 20-odd teams are committed to either holding a place near the front of the bunch or trying to improve their 〉

Tirreno-Adriatico, the Italian 'Race of Two Seas', takes place in early March and is one of the first markers of form for the peloton's stage race specialists

Crosswinds can whip up quickly, splitting the peloton, with smaller groups of riders forming echelons. This can result in time gaps or extreme efforts to get back together

JARGON BUSTER
ECHELON

The formation created as riders fan across the road when the wind is blowing into them, from the front and side. Although it comes from French, the French themselves tend to use the word *bordure*.

"Riders from the lowland countries of northern Europe deal better with the wind"

PRO'S PERSPECTIVE

"GET ON!"
Jack Bauer

"When an echelon starts forming it's akin to a train leaving the station. You hear riders saying, 'Get on! Get on!' If you can grab hold, jump on and get on the wheel, then... WOOOMMMFFF!! You get sucked along, you're on board. And if you don't, as soon as you touch the wind when that wheel has gone, then you're back to the next echelon. It happens so fast."

position, handling skills are vital. As is having an intuitive feeling for the ripples and waves of movement within the peloton, for predicting where a gap is likely to open before it's appeared, for knowing how the individual riders around you are likely to move.

RIDING IN THE WIND: BIG IS BEST

The wind is a divisive beast. Some riders, often the biggest and most strapping members of the peloton, are all jokes and smiles, relishing what's to come, knowing that they're likely to thrive. Others, generally those with something significant to lose such as GC contenders, are apprehensive, knowing that fate could turn against them without them being able to do much about it.

Like the often-made assumption that the best climbers come from more typically mountainous regions (Colombia, Spain...), it's generally presumed that riders who come from the lowland countries of northern Europe deal better with the wind. And that's probably not far from the truth. Belgian and Dutch riders have to learn from a very young age about how to look after themselves in windy conditions, which are a regular fact of racing and training life for them. At the same time, riders from other countries who make the northern Classics their focus are by necessity adept when the wind blows, as are the teams that tend to dominate those races, including Jumbo-Visma, QuickStep-Alpha Vinyl in the men's WorldTour and SD Worx in the women's.

Inevitably, riders who want to avoid being caught out if the race splits in the wind need to be close to the front of the bunch. Now that teams send staff ahead of the race armed with the latest satellite images and weather reports as well as state-of-the-art anemometers, the riders and their directors have a good idea of the wind direction and its speed throughout. This makes it inevitable that there'll be a huge fight to be in the vanguard of the peloton at those moments when the impact of the wind is most likely to bite. This scenario will occur when the wind starts to gust with significant force across the direction of travel, causing the classic echelon effect in which riders fan out across the road in order to remain in the lead of the rider ahead of them in the line. A front echelon will form when the diagonal line runs right across the road from one kerb to the other, at which point the riders who don't make the first cut have to form a new echelon behind, and so on.

Once it's formed, an echelon essentially works like any pace-line. The rider at the apex does their turn, then eases off and, having sheltered briefly behind the riders in the line (going on the 'protected side' as they drop back), slots in at the end, the chain rotating seamlessly. More common and not as attractive as the 'migrating geese' aspect of kerb-to-kerb echelons are those instances when the high speed that's being set by riders rotating at the front of the bunch strings out the peloton behind them in one snaking line. When a rider in that long chain drops off the wheel in front, usually because they're tired and the intensity of the pace is too much for them, it's almost impossible for any riders behind to jump across the gap as it begins to open.

LEADING OUT A SPRINT

Until the mid-1950s and the emergence of Rik Van Looy's 'red guard' at the Faema team, sprinters tended to rely on their own natural talent to seek out success. But, as the level and depth of competition increased, sprinters increasingly came to rely on an organised and rapid lead-out by riders who could lead into the final 200 to 300m, where they could make their final acceleration. This approach became even more specialised in the late 1980s at the Dutch Superconfex team, managed by Jan Raas. Rather than relying on two or three riders leading out their sprinter, Jean-Paul van Poppel, Raas provided the Dutchman with five or even six strong riders, tasking them with chasing down any escapees and then keeping the pace high over the closing kilometres of a race, with the aim of giving van Poppel an 'armchair ride' into the finish.

In subsequent decades, the tactic was honed further still, notably by the teams built around Italian sprinter 'Super' Mario Cipollini and Mark 'The Manx Missile' Cavendish. The Briton's superlative lead-out 'train' was at HTC-Columbia, where the whole team would play a part in setting Cavendish up in the sprints. This would start with one or two riders setting a steady pace on the front of the bunch and gradually upping it to reel in the break.

Once the catch had been made, the other HTC riders would sustain the high pace, increasing it coming into the closing kilometres. Heading into the final kilometre, Cavendish would be sitting on the wheel of lead-out man Mark Renshaw. As the last of his HTC teammates pulled aside with 500m remaining, he ›

LEGENDS OF THE SPORT
FABIANA LUPERINI

If winning the Giro d'Italia Femminile a record five times wasn't enough to make 'Pantanina' an Italian heroine, being four-time national road race champion and a record five-time winner of the Giro del Trentino Alto Adige-Südtirol (back when it was a multi-day stage race) did the trick. But it was the three consecutive Grande Boucle Feminine victories (1995-97) that ensured Luperini's legendary status internationally.

> *"As competition increased sprinters increasingly came to rely on an organised lead-out"*

STAT ATTACK!
DOING THE SPLITS

Splits formed in the peloton as a result of echelons were the basis for Dan Lloyd's greatest ever triumph as a cyclist. Back in 2009 at the Tour of Qatar, he was part of the Cervelo Test Team which tore the race apart on a daily basis and catapulted Lloydy to the lofty heights of 4th place on GC!

WHEN ECHELONS CHANGE THE RACE

Once echelons have formed, which can happen extremely quickly, it's very difficult for riders to close the gap. But why?

Because if the bunch is already going fast, maybe 55kph, it'll require an immense effort on one rider's part to accelerate up to 60kph, even for a handful of seconds, to bridge the chasm that's opening. There's often a hiatus for a few seconds as the riders behind the split pool their resources and start to share the pace-making, hoping that the front group might ease off or that they can claw their way back up to the leaders.

There have been several examples of this occurring in recent editions of the Tour de France. In 2019, Thibaut Pinot and his Groupama-FDJ teammates went around the wrong side of a roundabout when the peloton was lined out in the wind on the stage into Albi. This left them well back in the hurtling bunch and unable to respond instantly when a gap opened ahead of them. Although they did manage to get within a few seconds of the lead group, they didn't have the firepower to complete the bridge. Pinot ended up losing 1'40" on GC. In 2020, Tour debutant Tadej Pogačar was among those caught out on the stage into Lavaur (not far from Albi), and lost 1'21" that day – but ultimately turned his deficit around in the stages that followed.

would hit the front, taking Cavendish up to around 65kph with 200-250m to the line, from which point the Manxman would accelerate further still, his final kick usually delivering the reward all that work had been designed to achieve.

After Marcel Kittel had snatched Cavendish's place as the sport's top sprinter, his Argos-Shimano train proving highly effective in preparing the German powerhouse for bunch finishes, the nature of sprints has changed. Rather than just two or three sprinters and trains dominating, a whole squadron of fastmen have emerged at the same time, including Sam Bennett, Fernando Gaviria, Caleb Ewan, Fabio Jakobsen, Arnaud Démare, Wout van Aert, Elia Viviani and Dylan Groenewegen. This has not only made sprints more competitive, but also far more unpredictable and has resulted in a significant tactical shift for those teams who put sprint stage victories amongst their objectives. This has also made it more interesting for spectators. (See more on p222.)

THE ART OF THE BREAKAWAY

Like the most successful sprinters and climbers, breakaway specialists hone their skills by trial and error. Thomas De Gendt, the best of these *baroudeurs*, or adventurers, as the French describe them, has said that there is no such thing as a so-called 'kamikaze' break because the riders in them should derive useful experience and knowledge even from an escape that's almost doomed to failure. According to the Belgian, who has won stages in all three Grand Tours, a canny breakaway rider will get an insight into the strengths and weaknesses of their fellow escapees, including which of them are strong on climbs, if they're lacking on descents and whether they're quick in intermediate sprints or coming out of corners. This, says De Gendt, is an unparalleled opportunity to observe if a rival rider will be useful in a break, in terms of their commitment to collaborate and work, and how best to outwit them should that occasion arise.

At the same time, breakaway riders can also appraise how the peloton reacts and can be controlled when it's chasing behind a group of escapees. It may seem odd that a small group of riders can manipulate a much larger and, when a pursuit is full on, faster-moving bunch of riders. Yet, on certain occasions, the riders in the breakaway are able to use the few cards they do hold to significant ❯

PRO'S PERSPECTIVE

TT MAN IN THE BREAK
Alex Dowsett

"If I go into a breakaway, I know it's a comfortable place for me because I know it's going to be a sustained effort, which is something that I'm better at than most. And I think your opponents respect that ability, which helps – you're known for being able to go fast for a long time, so you have that intimidation factor. And then if you're a time triallist like me who's into the equipment side of things, you know how to optimise your equipment to go faster. I think other cyclists fear that in you as well in road racing. They know that you'll have the faster set-up, that you'll have done the homework, done your thinking and turned up to that race with the fastest skinsuit, the fastest aero socks, and so on."

"Canny breakaway riders get an insight into the strengths and weaknesses of fellow escapees"

Mørkøv and Cavendish know that the understanding between sprinter and final lead-out riders is vital to stage wins

It's great when it works, right? Even better when it's French national heroes Julian Alaphilippe and Thibaut Pinot chasing you down in the Tour de France... and they miss out by 6 seconds

Breakaway legend Thomas De Gendt enhanced his reputation at the 2019 Tour de France.

Stage 8 saw the breakaway specialist take a win for the ages, forming an early lead group before breaking free and holding off the late charge of Julian Alaphilippe. It was an immense effort and one we can enjoy an insight into thanks to Strava. Here's a snapshot of De Gendt's physiological and performance numbers that day:

200km
Length of breakaway

3,874m
Day's elevation

5h14m
Ride time

39km/hr
Average speed

311 watts
Average power output

advantage. The riders who want to make the break work and are determined to commit fully to doing that will be mindful of not allowing any of the other escapees an easy ride. In order to prevent them sitting on the back of the line or only coming through for brief turns at the front, breakaway specialists like Thomas De Gendt and Alessandro De Marchi will, for instance, speed up on climbs to stretch other members of the escape, or press hard on descents, forcing them to chase. As the two riders tend to be among the strongest riders in any break they make, their objective is to make that advantage pay, rather than have others use it against them.

DE MARCHI ON BREAKAWAY STRATEGY

"From the outside, I think people have a very different idea of the breakaway compared to what is really happening when you're on the inside of a break," says Israel-Premier Tech's Alessandro De Marchi. "Many times, people think that the breakaway has got no chance of making it to the finish. But, when you're in the break and you've got good partners with you, you never think that there's no hope of going the distance. You've maybe only got a small chance, but you go for it, you focus totally.

"Of course, there are times when breakaway riders don't really believe in their chances and you can see that they're effectively there just to show the jersey, and that's especially the case for the smaller teams. But even when I was with small teams, with Androni for example, I never got in the breakaway without having the belief that there was a chance I could win, because it made no sense to me to race like that, without really believing in something. I'd often end up with the wrong partners and arguing with them because they didn't believe in what we were doing, and sometimes that was frustrating. I've always committed because I believe that there's that chance of winning, otherwise I don't try.

"You always need to look at how the race might unfold, look at the parcours, try to work out where and how the bunch will probably arrive behind you. For example, the fact that there might be a tailwind is an important piece of information. If there's some part of the parcours where there's a tailwind, that can really change things. It can really help you when you're at the front because it's always harder for the bunch to catch you if you have a good tailwind. Climbs and descents ❯

"Specialists like De Gendt and De Marchi speed up on climbs to stretch other members of the escape"

On stage 19 of the 2018 Tour de France, Rafal Majka led over the Aubisque, only to be caught on the descent by Primož Roglič who took over the stage lead

After a 15km break, Alessandro De Marchi beat fellow Italian Davide Formolo in a two-up sprint at the 100th Tre Valli Varesine in 2021, with the chasing bunch led by Tadej Pogačar

near the finish change the situation too. If there's a climb in the final, you know that the bunch is probably going to speed up coming towards the bottom of it because the leaders' teams will want to be in a good position. That means you'll probably lose some of your advantage and you need to manage that so that you've still got enough of a gap to stay clear on the climb. You always need to be ready to adapt as the race develops, and, above all, to be aware of the parcours, because you can make the terrain work for you." (See more on p218.)

DESCENDING TO VICTORY

When trying to make a difference speeding downhill, the emphasis isn't so much on the DS's tactics, but more on the rider's audaciousness and skill. The best descenders will know exactly when and how hard to push, and will be able to do this at a point where they're likely to be right at their physiological limits while retaining their lucidity. Julian Alaphilippe is a prime example

> **"Julian Alaphilippe is a prime example of a rider who's adept at descending"**

of a rider who's particularly adept in this domain. His two-week spell in the yellow jersey during the 2019 Tour de France began with one of his trademark explosive attacks on the steep ramps of the third stage's final climb, but his success was cemented ❯

Geraint Thomas has had his fair share of crashes. Here, when riding with Team Sky he's about to get up-close with a telegraph pole on the way down the Col de la Rochette

DRAMATIC DESCENTS

Four of the fastest, most technically challenging downhills in road cycling make exciting viewing for fans

COL DE MANSE/ GAP

This twisty 9km descent tests the bike-handling skills of the world's best. Famously, in the 2003 Tour de France, Spain's Joseba Beloki crashed while Lance Armstrong took a detour down a grassy bank to avoid him. In 2015 on the nearby Col de la Rochette, Geraint Thomas hit a telegraph pole after a collision with Warren Barguil.

COTE DE PRAMARTINO/ PINEROLE

This sinewy tree-lined descent caused havoc at the 2011 Tour de France with a number of riders coming to grief. French rider Jonathan Hivert tumbled down a muddy bank while Thomas Voeckler, leader at the time, overcooked a corner and rolled onto someone's driveway. Thankfully the gate was open!

COL AGNEL

The Col Agnel's played host to both the Giro d'Italia and the Tour de France and tests even the best riders. The descent will bring back bad memories for Steven Kruijswijk: the Dutch rider ran wide and clipped a snowbank, the resulting crash causing a mechanical that all but ended his chances of winning the 2016 Giro.

POGGIO

The Poggio is climbed then descended near the finale of Milano-Sanremo. In 2022 Slovenian Matej Mohorič held off four attacks on the climb by his countryman Tadej Pogačar and launched an attack on the downhill. He used a dropper seatpost to enhance his superb bike handling and impressive bravery, drew out an advantage and held off the chasers to win.

Steven Kruijswijk's reign in the maglia rosa and dreams of the 2016 Giro d'Italia win came unstuck after clipping this mighty snowbank at the Col Agnel

PRO'S PERSPECTIVE

BANNING THE SUPERTUCK
Gino Mäder

"I was sad when they implemented the ban because, for me, it was one of the more comfortable positions and I felt safe. In the 'supertuck' I could see 100m ahead and judge where the road surface was good. The ban hasn't changed speeds when descending in the group, but when you're alone it's now significantly slower."

The Swiss rider Gino Mäder, one of the more exciting descenders, used the now-banned 'supertuck' position to great effect

by his daring on the following downhill, reading the ideal line into bends so that he wouldn't have to brake going through them, sticking out his knee and his elbow like a motorcycle racer.

Like most of his peers, Alaphilippe would also adopt the 'Mohorič position', perching on his top-tube in front of his saddle in order to improve aerodynamics, as Slovenian rider Matej Mohorič had done during the Junior World Championships in 2012. In early 2021, the UCI banned this 'supertuck' position on safety grounds, an initiative that received equal amounts of condemnation and praise. It has resulted in a return to the classic descending style, which demands that riders maintain three points of contact with the bike – on the bars, the saddle and pedals. This position may be less aerodynamic, but can still be extremely effective when it comes to opening or indeed closing a gap. Mohorič's subsequent descent of the Poggio in the 2022 Milano-Sanremo using a dropper seat-post was an eye-catching repost to the rule change.

HOW TO RACE ON THE COBBLES

Although the Tour de France does include cobbled sections of road from time to time, they're generally a feature of the northern Classics and stage races that take place in that same area. The most renowned – infamous even – are those that appear in Paris-Roubaix. These granite cobbles, or setts, were laid for the most part during the 18th and 19th centuries, although not in an even and very precise way as was the case on the Champs-Élysées in Paris or in other major cities.

Often rough and misshapen, worn by the elements and heavy farm machinery, they demand what at first seems to be the counterintuitive tactic of being attacked at speed. This enables a rider to judder along the top of the cobbled surface, and reduces the chance of wheels and tyres snagging on the sometimes-gaping cracks in between the stones. Classics specialists will also endeavour to ride along the crown of the road, primarily because the grit and small stones that are most likely to cause punctures collect in the worn sections that have been rutted by farm vehicles over many decades.

Watching riders tackling Paris-Roubaix's many cobbled sections, it also quickly becomes apparent that most of them opt to ride on the verge where this is possible, which reduces the juddering impact of the cobbles, although it increases the danger of encountering a flint-edged stone.

›

COBBLES CONUNDRUM

The polished pavé of the Champs-Élysées and the cutting cobbles of the rough roads to Roubaix offer a very different challenge. Tour de France champions who have performed at Paris-Roubaix are few and far between. Before **Bradley Wiggins** in **2015**, the last Tour champion to line up for Paris-Roubaix was **Greg LeMond** in **1994**.

INSTANT EXPERT
SUSPENSION SYSTEMS

While rider positioning and strength are the main factors in racing the Classics, tech also plays its part. With tyre widths and pressures, wheelbases and geometry changes all being tried to take the cobbles, it was the Z team who first introduced a mountain bike-style RockShox suspension fork, and won Paris-Roubaix in 1992 and 1993 with French rider Gilbert Duclos-Lassalle, triggering development from many teams and brands.

If there are no clean gutters, the ridge in the middle of the cobbles is the line of choice, with a bigger gear and higher pace favoured

Smiling or grimacing? Maybe both. 2015's Paris-Roubaix was 2012 Tour de France winner Bradley Wiggins' final race for Team Sky

Look weak when you're strong: Mark Cavendish used psychology to his advantage in Italian races in 2009

Look strong when you're not: Stephen Roche bluffed his rivals and buried himself in the 1987 Tour de France

TACTICAL TRICKERY

There are some devious tricks up riders' tactical sleeves – including bluffing their rivals

>> Revisiting Jean Stablinski's comment in Chapter 1 that riders should endeavour to appear strong when they're weak and to look weak when they're strong, there are some clever ways this can be achieved, and examples where it's worked wonderfully.

CAV ON THE CLIMBS

Mark Cavendish served up an exemplar of the Frenchman's approach as he prepared for Milano-Sanremo in the spring of the 2009 season at the Tirreno-Adriatico stage race that precedes it. The Briton made a show of struggling on the climbs on the harder days, prompting some rivals and commentators to suggest that he had no hope of coping with the small, but super-fast climbs in Sanremo's finale. Cavendish, though, was in great shape and when *La Primavera* reached its climax, he was not only in the bunch that swept down off the Poggio into the finish town, but was the only one with the speed to react when Heinrich Haussler jumped clear in the final few hundred metres, the Briton overhauling the Australian in the last few metres to take the title.

ROCHE PLAYS IT CANNY

Giving the impression that you're strong when you're at your limit demands immense willpower as well as nous. One of the key moments that enabled Stephen Roche to win the 1987 Tour de France title is often forgotten among the many famous incidents that shook up that race. It occurred on the crucial stage into Villard-de-Lans, where the Irishman ended up on the attack with rival Pedro Delgado, the pair of them among a group that had attacked race leader Jean-François Bernard earlier in the stage. On the final climb, realising that he was wilting, Roche rode up alongside the Spaniard, who was pressing hard, giving the impression that he was still strong. It paid off. Approaching the line, Delgado did sprint clear to win the stage, but it was canny Roche who pulled on the yellow jersey that afternoon and who eventually won the title.

FROOME'S PACE CALL

Thirty years later, Chris Froome resorted to a similar tactic in defence of the Tour de France title. On the key Pyrenean stage of the 2017 race to the steep finish on the runway at the altiport >

LANTERNE ROUGE

Refers to the rider lying last in the General Classification, the term referencing the red light displayed on the back of trains. This rider used to wear a black jersey at the Giro d'Italia, while finishing last at the Tour de France retains its own especially respectful renown.

On the 2017 Tour de France Chris Froome used his legs, head, and teammates to bluff the opposition and limit his losses

serving the Peyragudes ski station, Froome realised early in the stage that he'd made the basic error of underfuelling. With three passes to negotiate before the final haul up to the line, the Briton instructed his teammates to keep the pace high at the front of the bunch, maintaining the impression of strength and control that Team Sky had become renowned for.

On the last of those climbs, the Col de Peyresourde, Froome sensed he was weakening and asked his pace-setters to ease back a touch. "I started to feel really weak, I was close to blacking out," he said later. "I realised that if my rivals attacked I would have a serious problem because I wouldn't have been able to follow."

He escaped from this fate thanks to two things. Firstly, his awkward style on the bike, which makes it difficult for rivals to assess whether or not he's in good form, because he always looks like he's struggling. Secondly, he pulled out of his teammates' slipstream and deliberately eyed his rivals, making a show of sizing them up, a ploy that's often the prelude to an attack. The ruse worked. Although his rivals did attack, they waited until the final few hundred metres before they moved, only realising then – and too late – that Froome was unable to respond. Although he ceded the yellow jersey to Fabio Aru, the Briton's losses were minimal. Ultimately, he captured the title for the fourth time.   ❯

⦿⦿ JARGON BUSTER

DIESEL ENGINE

A rider who maintains a constant power output and speed, especially on climbs, rather than changing pace, even sticking to the plan when rivals do attack. This characteristic helped **Chris Froome** to his four Tour de France successes.

MONT VENTOUX

This 1909m mountain in Provence has featured regularly in the Tour de France and found status as an iconic climb. It has witnessed triumphs — such as Alberto Contador sealing his second GC in 2009 — tragedy, with **the death of Tom Simpson** from heat exhaustion in 1967 — and farce, with Chris Froome running in cleats to minimise losses after a crash on his way to eventual victory in 2016.

DOUBLE BLUFF?

*Conning your competition is an art form...
but it doesn't always work*

Bluffing your rivals by feigning pain and deep fatigue doesn't always work, as was highlighted by two incidents during the 2021 Tour de France. The first happened on the unprecedented double ascent of Mont Ventoux. The evening before, World Champion Julian Alaphilippe suggested that the stage was too tough for him, only to go on the attack almost from the moment the start flag was waved. The Frenchman led over Ventoux the first time, the first rider in the rainbow jersey to do this since Louison Bobet in 1955. However, on the second, more testing, ascent from Bédoin, he lost contact with the break, from which Wout van Aert won. "I wanted to try and give people something to savour, but it was a lap too far. On the first ascent I was good, but not on the second, which is a shame," Alaphilippe confessed.

Days later, Richard Carapaz's attempt to sandbag race leader Tadej Pogačar on the summit finish at the Col du Portet came to nothing when the Slovenian sussed the Ecuadorian. As the pair went clear with Jonas Vingegaard on the Pyrenean climb, Carapaz sat on the back, not contributing to the pace-making, trying to give the impression that he was only capable of holding the wheels. As their Team Ineos rival sat in, responding to each injection of pace, Pogačar and Vingegaard exchanged a few words. "He said to me he thought Carapaz was bluffing, and I knew it also. It was nothing unusual, this is the tactic in cycling. Then he tried to attack," Pogačar revealed after the stage.

TECHNOLOGY IN TACTICS

How the development of technology has changed, and continues to change, race tactics

>> Much like Formula 1 motor racing, technological development has always been a fundamental part of bike racing, as well as being a constant topic for discussion and, in some cases, disagreement. Going back to the sport's early days, Tour de France boss Henri Desgrange assiduously applied rules that he believed would ensure that the strongest racers would prevail and which included the suppression of the use of derailleurs until the mid-1930s. He felt introducing them and giving riders the chance to use more gears would skew the competitive playing field to the extent that less talented racers might win. Interestingly, when the ban of derailleurs was eventually lifted in 1937, the gaps between the best riders and the rest increased significantly, illustrating how wrong Desgrange's dogged refusal to allow them had been.

THE ROLE OF RADIOS IN RACING

Fast forward to the current era and similar debates are ongoing, most often regarding the use of radios and power meters and what is seen as the significant and, to some, the injurious influence they have on racing. Radios have been used in the peloton for almost three decades now, allowing two-way communication between rider and directeur sportif, and, as the technology has improved, have become a standard part of a racer's kit, with the receiver/transmitter usually slipped into a tiny pocket on the inside back of team jerseys.

The argument against their use essentially boils down to one issue – that they're seen as a way that team directors can direct their racers without the athletes having to make tactical decisions themselves. In short, they dilute the pureness of racing as a competitive contest. The riders, it is said, are no more than puppets with the directors pulling the strings.

The counter to this is that it's simply not valid. Those in favour of radios agree that tactics can be discussed and orders given from the team car to riders out on the road. However, they point out that directors and other staff in team cars often have very little idea what is happening up ahead on the road, and that much of the information that's provided is designed to ensure safety.

INSTANT EXPERT
TEAM RADIOS

Motorola was the first team to introduce radios in the early 1990s, what were then quite bulky devices produced by their principal sponsor. They have been met with criticism from some fans and media, and attempts from the UCI to ban them, including a ban announced in 2015 and swiftly overturned after pressure from teams. No radios are allowed in Olympic races, putting more emphasis on rider decisions.

Alberto Contador, Chris Froome and all the other riders now use team radios, but it was the Motorola team — formerly 7-Eleven — who introduced them to the peloton

Bearing in mind that races often take place on roads where traffic-calming measures such as speed bumps, narrowings, poles and barriers have been employed, riders, they affirm, need to be aware of these obstacles.

THE RISE OF THE POWER METER

If the use of team radios looks like it's here to stay in the top levels of cycling, in recent seasons, the use of power meters has arguably become even more contentious. Initially used primarily as a tool to optimise training, enabling riders to follow the training plans laid down by their coaches, they're now used by most racers during competition. This enables the capture of useful data that can be used, for instance, to instruct tactical decisions. But it has also been widely suggested that by giving riders and the team staff tracking them the ability to assess data on the ❯

"Team directors can direct racers without the athletes having to make tactical decisions"

move, they can suppress spontaneity and encourage uniformity, resulting in a less attractive racing spectacle.

Team Sky were depicted as the main culprits, critics highlighting the way their 'train' of mountain domestiques would set a consistently rapid tempo on the climbs, crushing the chance of unpredictability and panache in the process. "If you've got a team like Sky riding a certain tempo on a climb with five riders on the front, it's actually pointless attacking because you'll be going nowhere," Matt White, then the DS at Orica-GreenEdge, explained when the British team were in their pomp, guiding Bradley Wiggins, Chris Froome and Geraint Thomas to six Tour de France titles in seven seasons.

SHOULD POWER METERS BE BANNED?

There were calls from leading riders such as Alberto Contador and Nairo Quintana and from organisers such as Tour de France boss Christian Prudhomme for power meters to be banned from racing. However, they've gone unheeded, largely because it's always extremely difficult for any sport to row back from technological advances such as these. Through training all of the time with a power meter, riders naturally became much more aware of their own physiological sensations and, as a consequence, can often race as if wedded to the numbers on the power meter, even though they're not even glancing at it.

A stronger argument against those calling for the use of power meters to be limited or even banned from competition has come from the riders themselves in the form of a more aggressive, eyeballs-out style of racing that has restored panache and flair. This approach is encapsulated by the likes of Julian Alaphilippe, Mathieu van der Poel, Wout van Aert and Tadej Pogačar. Each of them races on feel, looking for the right moment to make their move, then seizing it wholeheartedly, no matter the risk involved. What's more, their all-or-nothing method has been contagious, as other teams and riders have realised that they have to race in the same way if they want to win the biggest titles.

Team Ineos, the successors to Sky, have followed this trend too, implementing a more adventurous attitude in the wake of Tao Geoghegan Hart's unexpected but brilliant 2020 Giro d'Italia win. "What I liked about this is, we've done the train, we've done the defensive style of riding and won a lot doing that, but it's not as much fun, really, compared to this, is it?" said Ineos Grenadiers

PRO'S PERSPECTIVE

TECH AND SAFETY
Matt White

"Obviously I've seen comments from Chris Froome and others saying that the racing's more dangerous now because everyone uses technology, and it's true. Years ago we didn't know what was in front of us, so we had to adapt on the fly. Actually, tech has made it a more nervous and dangerous experience because everyone knows exactly what's coming up. I know some teams do use it much better than others, but if everyone knows there's a dangerous point coming up, people end up racing to that dangerous point. Whereas in times past, you'd come to a dangerous point and you'd just get on with it, and there were fewer crashes because people weren't as nervous."

Power meters with sensors in cranks are commonplace in the pro peloton, but should they be? Marco Pinotti maintains there are arguments for and against them

general manager Dave Brailsford after that victory. "At the end of day, the sport is about racing, it's about emotion and the exhilarating moments of racing, and that's what we want it to be."

We asked six-time Italian TT champion Marco Pinotti if removing power meters would change much. "In time trials it would change things, but on the road I really doubt that it would have much effect. It might change performance in TTs, potentially increasing the gap between non-specialists and the specialists, because the latter have a natural feeling for pacing. But I don't think it would change much in road racing, partly because you can have other metrics that measure effort — you can't take away the use of speed, for instance. So, if you know a climb and know that you go up it at a certain speed, then you're still able to judge power to a significant extent.

"Van der Poel, Van Aert and Pogačar race on feel, looking for the right moment to move"

"I'd be curious to see if banning them did change anything, in the same way that banning radios wouldn't change much either. Another thing to bear in mind is that a lot of riders now are racing on feel, rather than watching their power meters. Racing's becoming more instinctive again."

❯

DATA IN PRO CYCLING
How data analysis is used in bike racing

>> Ever since Billy Beane turned around the fortunes of the well-backed but underachieving Oakland A's baseball team with a statistics-based sabermetrics approach that transformed the team's recruitment and tactical strategy, other sports have tried to emulate it. US entrepreneur Bill Stapleton took over the T-Mobile team in 2007, with a lavish budget but a string of doping scandals that led to the telecoms giant withdrawing.

Over five seasons, Stapleton turned the Columbia- and then HTC-sponsored team into the most successful in the sport, bagging close to 300 victories and bringing through a host of talents, headed by sprinter Mark Cavendish, all-rounder Edvald Boasson Hagen, time triallist Tony Martin and GC leader Tejay van Garderen. Stapleton didn't so much draw on stats as on the collective knowledge of his staff when it came to recruiting riders and deciding on strategy. The American team hired internationally, because bringing in directors and riders from lots of different countries provided an insight into other talents emerging in those nations, and helped to prevent cliques forming.

TEAM SKY PUSHED THINGS FORWARD
As Stapleton's team bowed out at the end of 2011, Sky emerged as the dominant force, establishing a group of Grand Tour riders that would win the Tour de France title seven times in eight seasons with three different riders. Its head, Dave Brailsford, recognizes that he was inspired by Beane's approach, while also admitting that he became obsessive at times in combing through cycling stats sites such as cqranking and procyclingstats, assessing the results and form of riders who might fit into Sky's structure. Slipstream boss Jonathan Vaughters is another devotee of these sites, in his case because his team's limited budget meant it was useful, vital even, to identify talent on its way up.

More recently, Team Dimension Data, supported by Japanese tech company NTT, adopted a more Beane-like approach to recruitment, team and race selection and strategy. NTT had already been providing on-screen stats to races, but pushed this focus further when it became the team's principal sponsor

PRO'S PERSPECTIVE

TECH AND THE DS
Cherie Pridham

"In the car there's a lot going on. We need to focus on the TV, on race radio, on the rider communications, on car-to-car communications. There are such intricate details on Velo Viewer, which makes our job a lot easier, because the planning that we do includes putting the points in on Velo Viewer that are critical on every stage – almost every corner, every roundabout, every narrow section. So the preparation before is probably a lot harder than it is when you come to the race itself. It's the modern way of racing and I really enjoy it. There are no easy races, no training races, no preparation races. Every race is important. We have to be prepared as if each one is our last race."

"Stats enable them to 'find the individuals that are overlooked in the system'"

Technology, tactics and talent helped position HTC-Colombia as the strongest team of its time

💬 **JARGON BUSTER**

SOIGNEUR

A French word translating as 'carer', *soigneurs* do a host of jobs, principally giving massage to riders after racing, but also preparing food and making up bottles, which they hand out in feed zones.

in 2020. Using artificial intelligence, machine learning and data analytics, NTT created what it dubbed Moneywheel (a nod to the book *Moneyball,* about Beane's work with the basketball team).

Moneywheel's results were mixed. Data forecasts suggested that the 2020 NTT roster should win 25% more points than the 2019 line-up, moving them into the top 15 in the UCI's ranking. Ultimately, they finished just four places higher in 20th having won eight races compared to seven in the previous season. The data and algorithms had, it appeared, produced a bounce, but only a small one. Yet, although the gains were insignificant in this instance, this type of analysis is sure to increase within cycling as teams attempt to spot and sign up the next big thing, and then try to ensure they get the best out of those talents.

CHAPTER 7 – HOW RACES ARE WON
IN A NUTSHELL

Much has changed since Henri Desgrange wrote the sport's first training manual in the late 19th century – but winning remains all about making the best of the resources in your head and your legs. Racing demands strength, but also cunning and the ability to judge your own resources as well as those of your rivals. ❯

ONE-DAY RACE TACTICS

*Ineos Grenadiers' **Michał Kwiatkowski** on his
'no tomorrow' approach to one-day races*

"I really love Classics as there's no tomorrow when you race
them. It's all on the day. Because of that, I always go into races
with the mentality of giving everything and maybe that happens
to be the best thing for me, given my abilities. When it comes
to stage races, I've obviously won quite a few in the past, but in
stage races you have to think very carefully about what's coming
the next day and the next week, you have to think of the long-
term and try to preserve your resources when you can. But when
it comes to the Classics and full-on racing for 250km, as it was in
Amstel Gold when I won it [in 2022] and as it is in other races like
[Paris-] Roubaix, they perhaps suit me better. I've some wonderful
experiences in the past in one-day races, and I've learned from
many different riders, great champions, riders who always had
high ambitions and always went out to win the great Monuments
of the sport, and that's inspired me a lot.

"I do have some regrets about not racing some one-day events
like Roubaix earlier in my career. I think it's a pity that because
the body has its limitations you can't combine so many great
races. I think that the combination of the Ardennes and cobbled
Classics is always a tricky one to get right, especially when you
take into account that with the likes of Strade Bianche and Milano-
Sanremo, there are so many nice races in the calendar. As a
consequence of this, you have to pick the right ones for you and
it's always a hard choice. You do that based on the experiences
you've had — what went wrong, what went well. You can change a
little bit but not completely because then things can go wrong.

"Looking at the overall strength of our team, you have to be
confident, and you have to have belief in your own abilities. We
go into the Classics without a pure leader, because we believe
in the strength of the team, we believe in the fact that tactics can
play a key role and that we have nothing to be afraid of."

Michał Kwiatkowski
Double Polish road and TT
champion, 'Kwiato' was 2014
Road World Champion and
boasts Milano-Sanremo (2017),
Amstel Gold Race (2015,
2022), E3 Harelbeke (2016),
Clásica de San Sebastián
(2017) and Strade Bianche
(2014, 2017) on his impressive
one-day palmarès.

After soloing into Sienna at the 2017 Strade Bianche, Kwiatkowski beat Peter Sagan and Julian Alaphilippe in a three-up sprint to claim his first Monument at Sanremo

2022 saw Kwiato claim his second Amstel Gold Race victory – this time from Benoît Cosnefroy (left) by the narrowest of margins

After losing time early in the 2020 Tour de France, Richie Porte took opportunities to claw it back later, earning his place on the final podium

PRO'S PERSPECTIVE

STAGE RACE STRATEGY FOR GC

*Trek-Segafredo Directeur Sportif **Kim Andersen** shares his experience on managing a flexible GC strategy*

"Riding for GC is a case of having an overall strategy, a plan that you work out beforehand, and then adapting that, day-to-day. In the last season that Richie Porte was with us at Trek-Segafredo in 2020, he was up there on all of the key stages where you'd expect the GC battle to be decided and finished third overall, but lost some critical time in the crosswinds on a stage at the end of the first week — which of course you don't plan for but is exactly one of those things that can always happen and means you have to make adjustments to your plan. When everything's going well in a stage race, it's easy to be a DS, but it's on days like that where things don't go your team's way that you earn your money. Your job then is to get your riders to try to believe in themselves again.

"Nowadays teams are able to measure everything, so they know more or less about the riders' condition and form, what the roads are like, the gradients, the wind direction and strength. These are all important. But I think the critical thing for the GC guys is to avoid expending energy when they don't need to. They need to be as fresh as they can for the key days. At the same time, the GC riders need to ensure that they don't use up their teammates' resources too early either, that they don't push them to exploding point until the critical moments. It's a delicate balancing act. You've got to be very adaptable, whether you're the GC leader, or the DS or support rider who's trying to help them make a success of the plan that's in place."

Kim Andersen

As a professional rider throughout the 1980s Andersen won GC at his home Tour of Denmark, stages at the Tour de France and the Vuelta a España, and La Flèche Wallonne. After moving into management in the 1990s he is now one of the most experienced team directors in the sport.

PRO'S PERSPECTIVE

MAKING THE BREAKAWAY WORK

*Israel-Premier Tech's **Alessandro De Marchi** explains how the break can outwit the peloton, and then, how to outwit fellow breakaway rivals*

"For the breakaway to outwit the peloton has become difficult in recent years because there aren't that many guys who are smart enough or have enough experience to say, 'OK, now we're going to play the peloton. We'll try to trick the bunch by slowing down and then speeding up'. In the last few years, I've had to spend time explaining that if we don't adopt a strategy like this then we wouldn't have a really good chance of staying clear. I'd say to the other guys, 'Look, if we slow down for 15, 20, 25km, we'll save some energy and then we'll be able to drive harder in the last hour or hour and a half.' At that point, you have to go full gas.

"Once you understand that the peloton will never really let you get a big gap, you need to play with them a bit. If you slow down, they'll probably slow down too because they don't want to catch you too soon. By doing this, you can then increase your advantage because when you speed up, it always takes the peloton a little while to respond. This enables you stay clear for a few more kilometres, and that's good because that means you get closer to the finish. Even if you only have a small gap, by getting closer to the finish and having saved a bit of energy, you've got the chance to put that energy to good use in the last 40-50km.

"At that point, you might also get a bit of a tailwind perhaps, some small thing that can change the contest in your favour at the last moment. But you need to be smart and be prepared for the fact that they don't always slow down. But sometimes it can work. The last time it almost worked out was at the Critérium du Dauphiné in 2019. It was a really easy stage, a sprinter's stage, and we were three good guys in the front. We almost tricked the bunch that day, but I got caught inside the final kilometre.

Alessandro De Marchi

One of the pro peloton's most experienced riders, the Italian is admired for his attacking mindset and wilingness to get in the breaks that work, not least the hilly stage 7 at the 2014 Vuelta a España when the break outwitted the bunch and he outpowered his escape companions.

Alessandro De Marchi, then riding for CCC, nearly made it stick at the 2019 Critérium du Dauphiné

"You need to be aware who is with you in the breakaway, firstly because you need to know if you'll be able to count on strong support, because when it gets towards the end and you're looking for a result you always need to have good cooperation in a small group. You need to know which of the guys are strongest and which of them are probably going to run out of gas after, say, 200km. Then, when it comes to the finish and fighting it out for the victory, you have to study all of the other guys and suss out how they're going, whether they're good on climbs, on descents, whether they take a good line through corners.

"I often struggle a bit in the beginning and many of the other guys are a bit stronger. But once you get near the finish after, say, 200km and five hours of racing, that balance changes and you need to be ready for that, to notice how riders are responding and probe the weaknesses that you think you've spotted."

PRO'S PERSPECTIVE

RACING IN ECHELONS

*Dutch former national road champion, and winner of Kuurne-Brussel-Kuurne, **Fabio Jakobsen** knows how to win when the wind blows!*

"Coming from the Netherlands I've always ridden in the wind. Echelons are what I've been doing since I was 12 years old, so, I kind of do it on instinct. As a sprinter, you need to be a bit lazy because you need to save energy where you can. But, on the other hand, you need to focus on positioning and sometimes sprinting to make sure you're in the first 10, 15, 20 riders, and especially when there's a crosswind. When you're in an echelon, you need to keep going through to the front, because if you are in the gutter at the end of the line and there is a swing in the middle of the group that's where the crashes happen. I would say that coping with crosswinds is 50 per cent focus and knowledge of the route, and the other 50 is just having the condition in the legs.

"Me and my teammates always pay attention to each other in crosswinds because you can let each other in if echelons start to form. We yell each other's names. If you're the first one from the team in an echelon and there's a teammate in front of you, you yell his name so that he can slot in ahead of you, and you try to do that with as many guys as possible.

"It looks like chaos but, in the end, it's controlled chaos because an echelon also needs to work together. So there is some kind of cooperation and then we try to stick together. It's not always possible, but ultimately there needs to be teamwork to stay in an echelon like that."

Fabio Jakobsen

Twice a winner at Scheldeprijs, sprint specialist Jakobsen knows how dangerous pro cycling can be, having suffered life-threatening injuries in a crash in with Dylan Groenewegen sprinting in the 2020 Tour of Poland. He has come back stronger, winning the 2021 Vuelta a España points classification and 2022's Kuurne-Brussel-Kuurne.

Dealing with echelons comes with experience, and that's a part of Jakobsen's racing armoury

PRO'S PERSPECTIVE

LEADING THE LEAD-OUT

*QuickStep-AlphaVinyl's **Michael Mørkøv** on how the
sprint lead-out works... on paper, and in real life*

"I happen to believe that the perfect lead-out doesn't really exist.
Before every bunch sprint all the teams sit down and make a
plan. They decide who will pull, where, for how long and how
hard. That's the easy part. The hard part is to do it in real life. In
my experience, bunch sprints never go as planned. I would say
that things go perfectly in those moments when you get all the
guys that you expect into play. So, if you've planned that in a final
you'll go in with five riders and all five manage to be there at the
right moment and cover the sprinter, that's the perfect scenario.

"Sometimes you get the help of other teams or maybe you
just take advantage of them. I think the most perfect moment
in a lead-out, because it highlights the degree of last-minute
understanding, is when you manage to have an advantage in
speed on the other teams. That's when you can hit the jackpot,
when you can make the sprinter who's not the fastest win against
sprinters who are very fast. As a lead-out, you manage to make
that difference through your speed, through your acceleration.

"Today, usually in WorldTour races, teams are much more
organised. Hardly anyone is allowed to go on breakaways
now. I believe that's because each rider starts with a purpose –
protecting a GC captain, a role in the lead-out – and not only top-
line sprinters but also second tier sprinters often have full teams
to support them, with maybe as many as 10 teams competing to
do a lead-out. Obviously there's not enough space for everybody."

Michael Mørkøv

A multiple World Champion – and Olympic gold medallist in the Madison
– on the track, Mørkøv is multiple national champion on the road. For his
'trade' teams the Dane's prowess on the road has been as a sprint lead-
out specialist, notably for Sam Bennett and latterly Fabio Jakobsen and
Mark Cavendish, to devastating effect.

Irish sprinter Sam Bennett described Mørkøv as the 'best lead-out in the world' when they were teammates at Deceuninck-QuickStep

CYCLO-CROSS FORMATS AND TACTICS

Cyclo-cross has its own parcours, rules and regulations along with tactics – or at least techniques – for winning

>> At the elite level, cyclo-cross riders compete under national banners in UCI World Cup and World Championships races, and in trade team colours in all other competitions. Although team tactics can come into play, 'cross is essentially a discipline for individuals, where the strongest and most skilful riders prevail, assuming they can avoid – or at least minimise – crashes or punctures and mechanical breakdown. The UCI rules stipulate that courses should be on closed circuits that are between 2.5-3.5km in length, of which 90% is rideable, and be at least three metres wide throughout. There may be obstacles, including planks, steps and footbridges, and a variety of challenging surfaces to ride – and run – on is to be expected. Men's elite events must last as close to 60 minutes as possible. For elite women, the specified duration is 50 minutes.

CX TACTICS

Tactics in cyclo-cross have essentially remained unchanged since the discipline's founding in the early part of the 20th century. Unlike road racing, where the importance of drafting is paramount, the key to success in 'cross is to be at the front, the one position where you're guaranteed to be able to go at the speed you want and, crucially, take the line you want. If you're following wheels, you're almost certain to be hindered in terms of tempo or direction of travel, resulting in a steady loss of ground on the leading rider.

Technique also plays an important role in cyclo-cross. As well as being able to produce power and handle the bike in a range of conditions, vital skills include being able to dismount and remount smoothly, run with your bike on your shoulder over obstacles and over short but steep rises, and, above all, maintain a steady tempo through cloying mud or treacherous sand traps. The ability to push hard out of tight or even dead corners is another quality that's fundamental to success.

PRO'S PERSPECTIVE

ESPORT RACING TACTICS

Ashleigh Moolman Pasio

"Like gravel, eSport racing has quickly captured a large number of enthusiastic devotees, many drawn by the easy access it provides to the competitive environment and by physical test it provides. "There's no denying it, indoor racing is hard," 2020 UCI Cycling Esports World Champion Ashleigh Moolman Pasio told *Cycling Weekly*. "In road racing, there's always the worry that you might do too much and get caught by the peloton. Whereas in Zwift, you can put in an attack, go deeper until your legs are screaming. You can have the comfort that no one can catch you; there's no need for hesitation until you cross the finish line."

"The key to success in 'cross is to be at the front where you can go at the speed you want"

Cyclo-cross tactics are a blunt, and effective, instrument in comparison to road racing

Lucinda Brand

Dutch powerhouse and 2021 CX World Champion Brand has many World Cups and Superprestige wins.

💬 JARGON BUSTER

SHOULDERING

On steep, muddy sections and over some obstacles it's quicker to dismount and run — carrying the bike by balancing the underside of the top tube over the rider's shoulder.

PRO'S PERSPECTIVE

CX START IS VITAL

*Cyclo-cross World Champion **Lucinda Brand** shares the most important tactic for 'cross success*

"The start is extremely important. You need to be very quick off the start line in order to get a good position when the course narrows. The further back you are, the more riders you've got to overtake.

"When you inspect the course, you'll see where the difficult parts are and how important a role the wind will play, and as a consequence of that you might decide, for example, that it's better not to take the lead, but maybe take second position. But it's not like in road racing, where you can sit in the bunch drafting and going easy. If you do that in 'cross, you're definitely going to be held up somewhere, and then you'll need to chase, assuming that's even possible.

"The main rule is to keep out of trouble. Then, of course, you do like you do in road racing and look for the places where you are a bit stronger than the other riders, to see if you can attack there. But in certain races, it may be smarter to stay together a bit longer, in others you try to go alone as soon as it's possible. It depends really on the course."

True or false? Shorter riders are employed to provide a 'balance point' as taller riders follow mandatory wheelie practice on training camps

PELOTON SECRETS

Training secrets, odd things riders do, FAQs, the bare truths of bike racing... and what does it take to become a pro? Here's how it looks from inside the peloton

>> Cycling is the most democratic of sports, pitching up in locations large and small right across the world, drawing in spectators with its colour and clamour. The action and settings tend towards the spectacular – certainly in the biggest races that get the global TV coverage – and once fans are hooked on these, there are more hidden beauties to be discovered inside the men's and women's pro pelotons. From the outside, some of the activities, suspicions and protocols in cycling can seem baffling and sometimes plain odd. But here we delve behind the scenes with the big and weird questions that all fans want the answers to.

PRO CYCLING FAQ
How much do pro racers train?
Thanks to the logging and analysis of every ride, a precise answer can be given. In 2021, Bahrain Victorious's Matej Mohorič, winner of two stages at that year's Tour de France, rode a grand total of 30,697km, of which 11,913km were in UCI races. Ergo, he racked up 18,784km in training. Wout van Aert, a three-time Tour stage winner in 2021, racked up 31,064km on Strava. Although he didn't highlight the split between training and racing, according to Procyclingstats. com the Belgian completed 8,514km over 49 race days on the road in 2021. Those totals are around three times larger than an amateur who regularly rides three or four times a week, and would clock up somewhere around 10,000km of riding over a year.

Why doesn't Mark Cavendish win the Tour de France if he's the fastest racer?
With 34 wins after the 2021 edition, the Briton tied with the legendary Eddy Merckx as the biggest winner of Tour de France stages. Yet, ❯

while the Belgian claimed overall victories during his stellar career, Cavendish has always finished towards the back end of the field in Paris. Why? Because, rather than having the kind of huge all-round talent that enabled five-time champion Merckx to dominate the Tour, Cavendish's brilliance is entirely focused on delivering sprint finishes. Consequently, while he proved himself the fastest on four stages in the 2021 race, he regularly came in among the back markers in the mountains, losing considerable GC time. For Cav's objectives, this is neither a problem nor a disappointment. His consistently high finishes did pay dividends in the green jersey's points competition, though, which he won for the second time.

How do riders pee and poo when racing?

Evidently, no rider wants to stop when a race is full on, and all will do what they can to avoid this occurring. Pre-race adrenalin/nerves/ food and liquid intake means that racers' final action before riding to the start line is to head to the toilet on their team bus. Once men's races get under way, the peloton tends to stop in a spot during the opening kilometres where there aren't spectators so that everyone can relieve themselves again. A race leader stopping to pee is often another signal for the rest of the bunch to take a natural break.

> ### "On a flat stage of the Tour de France, the average rider would take in around 5,000 calories"

Although it's rare that a rider will be forced to stop by the pressing urge to poo, there are some well-known times when this has happened. On the stage into Futuroscope during the 1986 Tour that he eventually won, Greg LeMond defecated into a cap that one of his teammates handed to him when his stomach was upset by a dodgy peach. More recently, during the 'queen' stage of the 2017 Giro d'Italia, race leader Tom Dumoulin suddenly pulled to a stop and squatted in the ditch at the roadside to relieve himself, and then had to take up the pursuit of his rivals who had kept on racing. The Dutchman lost two minutes, but kept his overall lead and eventually took the overall title.

How many calories will a rider consume during a race?

On a flat stage of the Tour de France, the average rider would take in around 5,000 calories, more than twice the daily intake for the average male and two-and-a-half times the amount for the average woman, the majority of that being attributed to the day's ride. On a big mountain stage, the daily intake would almost double, reaching 8,000 calories or more. ❯

LEGENDS OF THE SPORT
PETER SAGAN

The only rider to win **three consecutive UCI road World Champion's titles,** the Slovak has a mighty seven Tour de France green points jerseys, five of them earned consecutively. He began as a mountain biker, winning his first rainbow bands as the 2008 Cross-country Junior World Champion.

STAT ATTACK!
COUNTING CALORIES

A study of Team Movistar at the 2015 Vuelta a España found the average energy expenditure during a stage ranged from 373kCal (1,560kJ) for the 7.4km TTT, and 1,090kCal (4,560kJ) in the 37.8km ITT, to 3,107kCal (13,000kJ) on flat stages, up to 4,707kCal (19,700kJ) in the high mountains.

In-ride fuelling is crucial, but anticipating a musette full of calories also helps riders punctuate long stages

Three legends: but as the expressions reflect, Mark Cavendish and Tom Boonen would have preferred Peter Sagan's gold to their silver and bronze medals

Weird things fans do: what goes through the mind of Groupama-FDJ's Stefan Küng when, mid-race, he rides past a 4-metre tall model of himself?

Not properly displaying a race number could land a rider with a fine, but turning the unlucky 13 upside-down? That's ok

What do pro racers eat for breakfast and lunch?
Breakfast, eaten three hours before a race starts to allow digestion and therefore optimum use of the calories taken in, is made up of carbohydrate-rich foods like muesli, cereal, fruit, smoothies, orange juice and perhaps even pasta or noodles to replenish energy-giving glycogen stores. On the transfer in the team bus to the start, they'll have a carb-rich snack such as a rice cake – which has become a staple of the pro peloton – and may be sweetened with honey or raisins.

On the bike, the riders will eat bite-sized snacks, bars and gels, and usually more of the latter as they get further into the race when the pace is high and it's a struggle to get solid food down. In recent seasons, the increasing stress on good and very precise nutrition has resulted in most teams taking on dietitians, who will often weigh out food for the riders to eat pre- and post-racing to ensure that they're getting exactly the quantities required.

WEIRD THINGS PRO'S DO!
Put a newspaper down the front of their jersey just before starting a long descent. A long-standing habit that's designed to prevent them getting a chill on the chest and falling ill.

Squeeze water out of their bottles going onto a climb. This is all about reducing the amount of weight you're carrying up the climb. Two full bottles weigh close to 1.2kg, which means expending a little more power to get that weight up the climb. Not carrying it at all is the simple solution.

Ice socks down the jersey. When it gets extremely hot, riders will often put an ice-packed lady's tight in just below the collar of their jersey and in between their shoulder blades in order to reduce their core temperature. Tights regulate the flow of the icy water, although we haven't established which denier number is the ideal.

Wear bottle-carrying vests. A relatively new innovation enabling a domestiques to carry several bidons from the team car back up to their teammates in the bunch without needing to stuff them all down the back of their jersey as was previously the case.

Pin the number 13 upside down on their jersey.
The superstition that this number is unlucky is as pervasive in the peloton as it is outside it. Accordingly, race commissaires don't mind this traditional reaction to being given this race number. ❯

INSTANT EXPERT
PRO CYCLING NUTRITION
Want to know more about cycling nutrition? Take some advice from one of the best in the business, former nutritionist to Team Sky and EF Education, Nigel Mitchell. He's written two books with GCN: *The Cyclist's Cookbook* and *The Plant-Based Cyclist*, both available now. See page 240 or gcn.eu/books

Paris-Roubaix winner Magnus Bäckstedt trained for power. He now shares his insight as a GCN+ commentator

PRO-CYCLISTS' TRAINING SECRETS

Strava, Zwift and social media can give us some insight into the stats recorded by some riders in training (as well as in competition), but here are some more traditional windows onto their world

▶▶ **Rohan Dennis** filled his innertubes with water in order to increase resistance and weight. It worked to a point, but he admitted it got rather messy when he punctured.

Matej Mohorič always chooses the lightest and fastest equipment for training. He says that this motivates him to go harder and faster when he's doing his race prep.

Ex-pro Magnus Bäckstedt took the opposing view to Mohorič. He trained on the heaviest bike he could get his hands on, for extra resistance, even going to the extent of filling his bottles with lead to add more bulk to his set-up.

Lizzie Deignan starts her pre-season training on 1 November. However, in order to regain her connection with the bike and focus on smooth pedalling, she doesn't start using a power meter until a month later. What's more, when she does then use the power meter, she's a good way towards full fitness and it's not as demoralising as it would have been using it from the start.

Tao Geoghegan Hart says that his key training session lasts for just 90 minutes and that he keeps his heart rate to between 85 and 90 beats per minute. It includes a mid-ride stop for coffee. That day is all about recovery following hard efforts in training and racing.

TT powerhouse and Grand Tour deluxe domestique Rohan Dennis has an unusual take on resistance training

PRO'S PERSPECTIVE

THE FUTURE?
Ashleigh Moolman Pasio *on
how eSports cycling will evolve*

"**I'm a huge advocate for eSports as a new discipline, because
I believe it has the greatest potential to globalise cycling. Road**
cycling is very Eurocentric, which makes it difficult for talented
riders from other parts of the world to enter into the pro peloton
– I had this experience first-hand as a South African, and I'm
faced with it every day with young South African female riders
who'd love to turn pro, but the number of obstacles they have to
overcome are huge. eSports has the potential to allow people
from other parts of the world to compete at the highest level.

"**So far UCI-level racing has only been on Zwift, which I think has
to change,**" she explains. "**I see the sport's different platforms**
becoming a bit like race organisations, so Zwift would be, let's say,
ASO [Amaury Sport Organisation, owner and organiser of the Tour
de France, Paris-Roubaix, etc], Ruvi is RCS [owner and organiser
of the Giro d'Italia, Milano-Sanremo, etc], and so on. There needs
to be racing on other platforms to ensure fairness and the healthy
development of the sport as a whole.

"**A big talking point is how to create an ISO-like standard across
the different platforms because there are discrepancies among**
smart trainers, and these become more apparent the higher the
level you compete at. These create challenges for the rider to get
to grips with the dynamic, because if they don't follow some kind
of logic or science when, for instance, you're doing a recon of a
course, then you only really get to understand the dynamic by
racing, which leaves you at a disadvantage.

"**In Premier League racing, you can change equipment, and
there are advantages from doing so, but at the highest level** of
competition they neutralise that aspect. But is there space for
changing tyre pressures, for instance, within eSports, depending
on the route and terrain? If so, how do they bring that into the
game? So there's a lot of stuff that's still happening in that space."

THE BARE TRUTHS OF PRO BIKE RACING

What's it like to be a rider in the men's or women's pro peloton? Here are some of the observations shared by riders on the inside

>> **Racing is easy.** Of course it's not, but at the same time, top level racers spend a lot of time riding at *their* cycling equivalent of walking pace.

Race hotels aren't great. There are clear exceptions, the most outstanding being the hotels at the UAE Tour. But on big events like the Tour they can be surprisingly poor bearing in mind 23 teams, their staff, the race organisation, members of the publicity caravan and thousands of media need to be accommodated in what are often remote and underpopulated areas.

Crowds are loud. At a packed event, especially one where there are a lot of kids shouting, the noise is louder than being in a nightclub or even a football stadium, primarily because the fans are within touching distance.

Race locations are dull. Not all of the time, but often starts and finishes are selected because of the space they provide for the whole race caravan. Consequently, remove the banners, barriers and finish line, and you'll often find you're in the middle of an industrial estate or close to a commercial centre.

Cycling is a team sport. There may only be one winner each day, but that lucky rider will have depended on the support of their teammates to some extent, often hugely if they're a sprinter who's called on a lead-out from most of their team to set them up and launch them towards victory.

Winning is the best feeling. Riders spend months and months training for these sometimes fleeting moments of success. When they do arrive, it's confirmation that the hundreds and hundreds of hours of preparation have been worth the effort.

While pelotons are large, race convoys and caravans are massive. There are two to three times as many staff working behind the scenes for the riders in a peloton, managing, massaging, mechanicing... At the biggest races, there may be the

INSTANT EXPERT

CX AN OLYMPIC DISCIPLINE?

Following road, TT, cross-country MTB, BMX Racing and most recently BMX Freestyle, Cyclo-cross is the next cycling discipline that may become an Olympic sport. The idea is for CX to feature in the Winter Olympics. The UCI first proposed it to the IOC (International Olympic Committee) in 2014 and it could potentially feature from the 2030 Games.

While snow-bound CX races are nothing new, the CX World Cup at Val di Sole, Italy, in December 2021 – with Elite races won by Dutch teenager Fem van Empel and Belgian multi-disciplinarian Wout van Aert – was a deliberately snowy showcase. Yet the Olympic charter mandating that Winter Olympic sports are held on snow or ice may still be an issue; a lot of CX is in the mud and some is dusty dry.

Orange-clad fans make the traditional Tour de France 'Dutch Corner' on Alpe d'Huez a unique party atmosphere, but the Team Sky riders press on regardless

same number again involved in race organisation, broadcast and other media activities.

Crashing doesn't hurt… That's true for the first 15 seconds after a rider goes down, but then it's pure agony. Riders may escape lightly, but if they've got severe gravel rash their wounds will require brisk scrubbing with a brush, then the application of bandages that are cumbersome and limit movement, but do help the healing process.

Fans in all places can get unrivalled access to their favourite riders. This became apparent during the first Tour de France in 1903 when the race left Paris to general indifference but found the roadsides packed when they went into the provinces. The same effect can still be seen today when races pitch up, often in towns and villages that are right off the professional sporting map.

With Cervélo TestTeam, Dan raced the Giro d'Italia twice, and the 2010 Tour de France

THE BIG QUESTION: WHAT DOES IT TAKE TO BE A PRO RIDER?

Watching the men's or women's pelotons stream by might seem like a world away, but they are actually human beings! Here's the inside line from the GCN presenters team on life as a pro cyclist

ABOUT Conor Dunne
First pro team An Post Chain Reaction
First pro race GP Marseillaise
Favourite race as a pro Milano-Sanremo
Palmarès highlight Becoming Irish national champion

For ex-pro and GCN presenter Conor Dunne there's one fundamental quality required to reach the top ranks and it's a simple passion for cycling. "Race because you love it, then take any opportunity you can get to race and don't be afraid to lose, to experiment and to push yourself beyond the limits you thought you had because those limits are undefined. But, most of all, enjoy it," Conor says. "Then, whether you turned pro or not, at least you can say, 'That was the time of my life'."

ABOUT Dan Lloyd
First pro team Team Endurasport Principia
First pro race Stausee Rundfahrt
Favourite race as a pro Ronde van Vlaanderen
Palmarès highlight Finding a contract!

Dan Lloyd suggests that innate qualities are paramount if a rider wants to become a cycling superstar. "Professional sport can be viewed as a pyramid in terms of the athletes competing," says Dan. "At the very top of the hierarchy are those riders who have the genes and therefore the natural talent, they've got all of the desire and motivation needed to push themselves in training, they are extremely competitive, they've got tactical nous, they're good at bike handling, and they're good at positioning themselves in the bunch. Then as you go down the pyramid, you get riders who've got most of those assets but not all of them."

As well as riding the Giro d'Italia and the Vuelta a España, Conor was 2018 Irish national champion

ABOUT Si Richardson
First pro team Plowman Craven
First pro race Tour of Ireland, 2007
Favourite race as a pro Tour of Ireland, 2007
Palmarès highlight Result: winning the Ras. But probably just making a living for 10 years from something I love so much.

Si's development in bike racing was multidisciplinary: as a Junior and Under 23 he raced cross country MTB and cyclo-cross, before signing pro terms for road racing. How did that help him? "At the time, I just did what I enjoyed, which kept me really motivated for both riding and racing at an age when a lot of more talented riders left the sport," reflects Si. "Road just didn't really appeal very much at that point and it seemed much harder to get into. In hindsight, I think taking a multidisciplinary approach was really beneficial in other ways too. Riding and racing off road pretty much guarantees a good level of bike handling ability which, as we know, pays off on the road, but physiologically too, combining disciplines seems to be incredibly effective. Most of all though, I think having a multidisciplined approach means that training and racing never get stale, there's always something different and exciting to do."

›

Riding for Trek-Drops, Manon hits the front racing in the HSBC UK Women's National Circuit Series in Otley, Yorkshire, UK

ABOUT Manon Lloyd
First pro team GB Olympic Development Programme
First pro race Junior European Championship
Favourite race as a pro Tour of California
Palmarès highlight World Cup winner and representing GB

Right Manon won the Madison and the Team Pursuit at the UCI Track World Cup in Glasgow, 2016

Below Now riding in GCN colours, Manon still pulls the legs off a group of international ex-pro riders

GCN Presenter Manon Lloyd, who was inspired by international track and road Olympic and World Champion Nicole Cooke, explains more about her time as a professional racer, and the experience of moving from international track duties to pro road racing and joining leading UK women's team, Trek-Drops.

"I loved both track racing and road, and switching between the GB track team and Trek-Drops was hard, two completely different disciplines within cycling," explains Manon. "My training on the track would be targeted to events just over 4 minutes long, on the road I needed to survive 3-4 hours of racing.

"A pro needs to be able to deal with pressure and being on the GB team is probably the most high pressure environment I have ever been in. Every single session is monitored, filmed, every quarter of a lap is measured in detail, every effort is de-briefed, your body measured on a regular basis. When you're having a good day on the bike that's fine, but on the bad days it can be hard to look at the stats knowing you can do better.

"Trek-Drops was the best UK women's team when I was racing. They looked like a team that always had a good time racing and I really wanted to ride one of the Miami Green Trek bikes – they're beautiful!

"I was lucky enough to have an agent who approached the Trek-Drops team owner, Bob Varney, and set up a meeting the day before the nationals on the Isle of Man. I remember having

"You train to be able to win, you make so many sacrifices because you want to win"

to sneak out of my hotel... it's all a big secret until you've signed the contract! The meeting went well but Bob told me that he had hundreds of emails from people wanting to be on the team. The next day was the national championships and thankfully I had a great race. I got in an early breakaway that stayed away until the finish, resulting in me getting 2nd. And Bob offered me a contract the next day!

"I raced because I loved cycling and I wanted to win. You train to be able to win, you make so many sacrifices because you want to win. I think, like any professional sport, you have to be selfish. You have to be good at saying 'no': no to friends' parties; no to family occasions because it clashes with a big race; no to day shopping trips because, as silly as it sounds, you can't be on your feet all day as it will affect your training. You become best friends with your teammates, but when it comes to selection for races it can be hard seeing your best friend on the sideline or at home, and vice versa."

ALSO AVAILABLE

ENDURANCE

How to Cycle Further By Mark Beaumont

GCN presents *Endurance* by the fastest person to ever ride around the world, Mark Beaumont. This complete 244-page guide to riding any distance – from 50 miles to a circumnavigation of the globe – covers everything from psychology, planning and bike set-up, equipment, to training and nutrition and much more.

ESSENTIAL ROAD BIKE MAINTENANCE

All You Need to Know to Fix Your Bike

260 pages packed with 71 step-by-step walkthroughs and 64 free companion videos across every aspect of bike maintenance, *Essential Road Bike Maintenance* is the ultimate, accessible and practical guide for road, gravel, commuter and hybrid bikes.

THE PLANT-BASED CYCLIST

Your Complete Guide to Plant-Based Cycling By Nigel Mitchell

The Plant-Based Cyclist is your accessible, complete and practical 244-page guide to plant-powered cycling. Whether you're just starting out on your cycling journey or are already an accomplished gran fondo or road racer, if you want to ride simply powered by the goodness of plants, *The Plant-Based Cyclist* will help inspire, equip and empower you to do just that.

Discover more from GCN books **gcn.eu/ books**

THE CYCLIST'S COOKBOOK

Food to Power Your Cycling Life
By Nigel Mitchell

Written by Nigel Mitchell, the acclaimed WorldTour cycling nutritionist, *The Cyclist's Cookbook* presents 67 of his most loved recipes. Covering the fundamental principles of how to fuel your cycling and insights into ingredients and equipment, the 244-page book brings together easy to make yet tasty everyday meals and snacks; indulgent celebration dinners and treats; pre-ride, on the bike, and post-ride recovery food and drinks, through time-crunched, healthy and nutritious 'fast' food — and everything in between.